Gertrude and Me

TONY BURKYS

ETT IMPRINT
Exile Bay

This edition published in 2024 by ETT Imprint, Exile Bay

Text © Tony Burkys 2024

ETT IMPRINT
PO Box R1906
Royal Exchange NSW 1225
Australia

ISBN   978-1923205-09-3   (pbk)

ISBN   978-1923205-10-9   (ebk)

Cover: Photograph of Tony Burkys and Gertrude by Ian Shadwick
Designed by Tom Thompson

CONTENTS

I had Gertrude 5

First Impressions 7

Snapshots of Glebe in the 50s and 60s 10

Meanwhile in Sheehy Street 12

Yeah! Yeah! Yeah! 14

Words and Music 16

A Tale of Two Bands 25

Verse... The Original Battersea Heroes 27

The Arts Factory 29

Chorus... Uncle Bob's Band 34

Coda ... Swansong 44

Pram Factory & Matchbox 47

Starting from Scratch 53

Balancing Act – Day Job, Family Life and Music 56

Sweet Atmosphere -The Café Society Orchestra 60

Music with Dave Clayton 67

West Ryde Primary School Band 71 - Crowle Home 72

Lonnie Lee & the Leemen 73

Modern Retro Sounds - 79

The Gentleman Callers - Ron Craig Studios 79

The Murray Hillbillies - John and Yuki 80

Jazz West - Cool Britannia 81

Eric Holroyd's Five Pennies - Them Were the Days... 82

Colourful Racing Identities 83

Guitar and Amps 87

Perils of the Road 93

Musical Fragments 97

Vignettes from the Bandstand... 102

Postscript 104

Acknowledgements 105

Website Links 106

B. B. King had *Lucille*, George Harrison had *Rocky*, Neil Young had *Old Black* and Willie Nelson had *Trigger* ...I had *Gertrude!*

Music is an ephemeral art form. It exists in the air and enters the brain via the ears. You don't look at it like a painting or photography, or read it like a poem or prose, or touch it like a statue, or wear it like jewellery, or walk through it and sit in it like architecture. You hear it in the air and after it enters the brain it stimulates the imagination in numerous wondrous ways. It can create colours, landscapes, dramas and emotions both profoundly melancholy and profoundly joyous. It can be triumphant or elegiac, majestic or wistful. It can also make the feet move. Just think of the staggering number of dance forms there are from a Swan Lake ballet all the way down to line dancing. Without music there is none of them. Certainly, in the theatre, some forms of choreography can tell the story on their own but generally speaking dance without music is movement without meaning.

A case could be made that some type of music is the earliest form of human artistic expression especially when you consider the aspect of dancing. Neanderthal, Denisovan and early Homo Sapiens did their cave paintings and ochre handprints but who knows when earlier Homo Erectus grunts became tuneful or rhythmic and premodern humans began moving to them, let alone picking up a couple of sticks or animal bones and inventing percussion … the Dawn of Man, the dawn of Drummers! I am tempted to say that some forms of modern music have a touch of Australopithecus Robustus about them … but this may be unkind.

This music that exists in the air and imagination is also different for everyone who hears it. We each have our own responses and therefore all are relevant.

There has always been world music or folk music and for hundreds of years now there has been classical music. But the distillation into different music styles that occurred in the 20th century is truly remarkable and for that America can take a bow. America did not pioneer all these different music styles, only most of them.

Other nations that contributed to 20th century popular music include calypso from Trinidad, reggae from Jamaica, Bossa Nova from Brazil, tango from Argentina and polka from Germany. But we can thank the great American melting pot of races for ragtime, blues, jazz, swing, country, rhythm and blues, rock and roll, rock, soul, folk rock and pop music that can include any of these elements.

There's a lot to like about music and this book is just the recollections of one music lover from way back and of the many kindred souls I have encountered in a lifetime of playing it.

Uncle Vlad playing the accordion in Klaipeda, Lithuania, 1965.

Eileen Mullins and Paul Burkys out strolling in September 1951 a few months before their wedding (with me on the way) - and looking like a Hollywood couple.

The Mullins clan outside Mick and Elsie's house in Forsyth Street, Glebe Point. Back row (l to r): Elsie, Auntie Von, mother, baby Michelle, Auntie Val. Front row (lto r): Uncle Mick, Uncle John, me, Dana, cousin Greg, Uncle Den, Mick Mullins - Pop.

FIRST IMPRESSIONS

Well then, I'll begin at the beginning. I never met my Uncle Vlad nor indeed any of my father's family in Lithuania. My father, Paul Burkys, came to Australia after World War II as a displaced person. Back then Lithuania was part of the Soviet Union and the Iron Curtain was firmly in place. I only knew the family on my mother's side, the Mullins clan in Glebe. This bloodline was Irish with a bit of English and Spanish thrown in the mix. They were not particularly musical although my mother, Eileen, could sing well, with Danny Boy being her specialty. And my uncle Den had a good collection of 78's which I sort of inherited and where I pinched a couple of swing era riffs from Artie Shaw's 'Gramercy Five' which ended up in some of my early songs. My mother remained a lifelong fan of Frank Sinatra, with his clear enunciation and true centre melody note pitching. My father was more inclined to bass/baritones like Paul Robeson with that marvellous depth and strength of tone. With either preference, there was a sound appreciation of good music. My sister Dana and I had this appreciation as part of our upbringing.

Another uncle, John Mullins, was a footballer and played with 'The Balmain Tigers' and the Newtown Blue Bags. I was very proud of him and even played a couple of seasons in the Balmain junior league before having to admit that I had the build of a guitar player not a footballer and while not being rugged I was fast, played on the wing and scored a few tries.

So, where did any musical ability come from? Even from a young age, I felt I was a bit different - a square peg in a round hole. I was also a difficult child, somewhat precocious and sometimes a bit nasty to my younger sister, who deserved none of this. I was jealous, perhaps, that someone was stealing the limelight.

My mother had to take me to a child psychologist at the old Camperdown Children's Hospital. The opinion was that I was highly strung. She was also told that I was more intelligent than many of the adults the psychologist was seeing and that the best thing was to keep my mind active and engaged. I then started getting books for birthdays and Christmas. Ancient History, palaeontology, sport and archaeology mainly. This did the trick and to this day, at age 71, they remain my favourite subjects, along with music.

Our family also bought an upright piano and I was sent off to piano lessons at a nearby girl's school, St. Scholastica's in Glebe, where for a year and a half I was rapped over the knuckles by a nun whenever my scales were not up to scratch. This of course did little to inspire any musical leanings although at my one and only exam I passed with honours.

The next step was to get me a cheap acoustic guitar to keep me occupied. I proceeded to teach myself which so far has been a lifelong endeavour.

My father would always say that although he could play a bit of piano and piano accordion and showed my sister Dana and me a few little chords, in his family his older brother, Uncle Vlad, was the real musician. So, any musical talent Dana and I have is inherited from him. I have one photo of Uncle Vlad on piano accordion accompanying a singer in Klaipeda Lithuania in 1965. His mouth is set in concentration and is a look I recognise I often get when playing guitar and, nowadays, double bass. I also retain a fondness for the accordion and many things European although I've never been there.

With my first guitar, 12. Don't know about any musical content but the stance is right.

When I was a toddler we got a puppy, Rudy, and for a few years we grew up together until he was poisoned by some local lowlife. Uncle Mick used to race pigeons and his pigeon coop was in our backyard in Sheehy Street, around the corner from Mick and Elsie's.

SNAPSHOTS OF GLEBE 50's and 60's

Glebe was largely working class back in those days, and for Dana and me, both our parents worked to make ends meet and we never went without. Glebe was also fairly conservative but this conservatism accompanied working class values. No privilege or entitlement here. In political terms I suppose you could call it old-school, right-wing Labor, Irish Catholic. At one end of Glebe there was the Harold Park trots and at the other end, the Wentworth Park dogs.

My grandmother, Elsie Mullins had one of the few telephones in Glebe Point and so she and her sister, Aunty Eileen, ran an SP Bookie operation from her house in Forsyth Street. On occasion I did a bit of 'running' for them delivering winnings and picking up losses, Dana also. Small scale illegal endeavours like this were generally accepted back then in Glebe, merely a part of life. There were also quite a few tough men around. Some renowned street fighters from families, as the saying goes, 'known to police.' But always an honour system was in place for the combatants. There were rules to be observed which went hand in hand with fisticuffs. My grandfather Mick Mullins, an Irishman, could get into a few fights up at the Toxteth Hotel and there was a story that one day he and a mate took on and won against a cricket team at the Bat & Ball Hotel at Moore Park. My uncle Den apparently also knew how to handle himself and was thus accorded proper respect. In Glebe, at times, you had to be good with your fists or swift with your feet. No wonder that I played on the wing.

With both parents working, I was usually given some coins to buy lunch from the school tuck shop but often these coins would end up in the pinball machine at Stone's Milk Bar next to The Astor picture show, later to become The Valhalla, on Glebe Point Road. As a result, I've never been overweight.

Cracker night in Glebe was quite an occasion. The next morning, we would prowl the back streets and laneways in search of any leftover bungers, fountains and skyrockets. These streets and laneways would be completely covered with the remains of fireworks.

Down at the end of Ferry Road next to the Glebe Rowing Club there used to be a timber mill and they had their logs floating nearby in the waters of Blackwattle Bay. A bit of a lark for us scallywags was to run along them hopping from one to another. Occasionally, you would slip into the water and the logs would close ranks above you. A panicked underwater swim to the end of the logs ensued. This only ever happened to me once and that was enough. No more log hopping. Besides, there were sharks in Blackwattle Bay.

One more memory comes from the summer months. There were many terrace houses in Glebe, in fact all houses were close to the footpath/street. Not much room for front yards. So, in summer the front doors would be open to get a through breeze down the hallway leading to the kitchen where 'Early Kooka' gas stoves would be cooking dinner. As you walked past these terrace houses you could guess what dinner was … grilled sausages with three veg. (mashed potato, peas/beans and carrots) … grilled sausages … ah! Lamb chops. On Fridays, most people ate fish in line with Irish Catholic protocol, pious or not. And while nowadays I mainly cook Chinese style food there are times when only sausages and three veg. will do.

MEANWHILE IN SHEEHY STREET

In the early 1960's we got a wonderful piece of furniture, a wooden laminated 3-in-1 on 4 tilted legs - TV, record player and radio. Valve powered of course.

Before then, we had a separate TV in the lounge room and on top of the fridge a valve Bakelite radio. I always remember turning it on then waiting for the valves to warm up before the sound slowly surfaced. Then as now certain songs just grabbed me irrespective of style. My first favourites were *La Mer* by Charles Trenet and *Ebb Tide*. The first rock and roll song I remember hearing on the radio was *Multiplication* by Bobby Darin. I thought he was brilliant as he did other styles as well from country, *Things*, to big band swing, *Beyond The Sea* (the English version of *La Mer*). There was also *Spanish Harlem* by Ben E. King, *Wolverton Mountain* by Claude King, *Summer Holiday* by Cliff and the Shadows and *I Remember You* by Australia's own Frank Ifield. But my number one favourite back then was *Wonderful! Wonderful!* by Johnny Mathis.

Certain sounds and instruments on these songs transported me to various places, along with the vocals. The drums on Multiplication emphatically said, 'here I am!' wherever that was. The marimba intro. riff to *Spanish Harlem* was a hot summer's day in New York. The glissando violins at the start of *Wonderful! Wonderful!* pictured strolling by the beach, before Johnny Mathis sang that was what he was doing. Hank Marvin's guitar intro for *Summer Holiday* was the sound of the holiday bus taking off, while the chromatic harmonica bringing in *I Remember You* just had an air of longing about it. *Wolverton Mountain* had some yodelling in it but it was the mystery 4th chord that grabbed my attention. Country songs normally only have three chords, in this case D, G and A, but the mystery chord, E7, with its unexpected jump up a tone, could have been part of a mountain ascent. So, while I could appreciate the lyrics, stories and singing on these songs, the musical components spoke just as clearly to me.

The TV was also a great source of music variety programs from '6 O'clock Rock', 'Sing, Sing, Sing' and 'Bandstand' to 'Sing Along with Mitch Miller' and even 'The Black and White Minstrel Show' (which is the only one where I would say I was too young to know any better). Later on, there was 'Kommotion' and 'Sounds.' I would also watch the ABC test pattern for its light classic program and where I first heard Elizabethan Serenade and Greig's Piano Concerto.

So from an early age I was naturally drawn to music that fired my imagination. I never stopped to consider how anyone else appreciated music only that my appreciation ran deep and quite possibly something was going to happen. In early 1963 that something happened.

YEAH! YEAH! YEAH!

1 - 2 - 3 - 4 - Bup Budup Bup Budup.

Arguably the most incendiary count in and intro. in the history of rock and roll and only surpassed by the same band a year later with possibly the most famous chord in music. A clanging G7sus4/A chord that startles the start of *A Hard Day's Night*.

This chord has long been debated and argued about. After many decades, I eventually worked out how to approximate the sound on a 6-string guitar. But to play it properly, you need a bass guitar note, a 6-string electric guitar, a 12-string electric guitar, plus George Martin, playing a cluster of notes on the piano. While the chord is based on a G7, there are a couple of extra notes that make it stand out … a C note in the guitars and a low A bass note on the piano.

The Beatles didn't invent powerhouse rock and roll intros. like this. They had heard Little Richard blasting into *Long Tall Sally*, Elvis powerfully pleading into *Heartbreak Hotel* and rock and roll's finest champion, Chuck Berry, scorching his guitar into *Johnny B. Goode*.

But for those of my age group, hearing this count in early 1963 was a clarion call we had never heard before. At age 10-and-a-half I sort of knew then that music was going to take over my life eventually. The Beatles changed everything for me. Pre-Beatles my interest was in individual songs by individual singers who followed the set guidelines of the music industry. The singer would sing a song written by a songwriter whose publishing company would push it to the record producer, who would then line up whoever was available from the ranks of professional studio musicians to make the record. This was how music was recorded. The industry was represented at every level with everyone making their living from it and everything sounding professional but similar. The Beatles sounded different because they wrote their own songs and they played their own instruments. On their first few albums only producer Sir George Martin joined in occasionally on piano. Session drummer Andy White was brought in for two songs on their first album as Martin was still a bit hesitant after not being impressed by former drummer, Pete Best. But it didn't take long for Ringo to become the indispensable drummer for Beatles songs.

And what songs! And what singing! Paul McCartney was equally at home with raucous Little Richard style R&B as well as ballads and show songs from musicals. John Lennon's distinctive timbre and authority made him the boss and when both voices combined it was excitement plus as well as textbook harmony influenced by but surpassing the Everly Brothers.

In June 1964, just before my 12th birthday in July, I saw the Beatles at Sydney Stadium on its revolving stage. I also remember the instrumental group, Sounds Incorporated, and Aussie/NZ rocker Johnny Devlin. My father took me along and it was hard to hear them as PAs of that time were rather primitive and the screaming was immense, but I was there to witness one of music's greatest phenomena. Shortly afterwards, the film 'A Hard Day's Night' was released and Beatlemania only increased its intensity if that was possible.

WORDS AND MUSIC

The Beatles had a profound effect on me going way beyond fan mania. The idea of writing your own songs came directly from them, especially when I learnt that none of them were schooled in music and just did their own thing. Natural talent that needed no qualifications. Of course I was inspired. Only the Beach Boys with their resident genius, Brian Wilson, writing all their music, could match them.

Later on, the lyrics of Bob Dylan brought an extra dimension, as did the songs of Crosby, Stills, Nash and Young, and Robbie Robertson and Richard Manuel with The Band. Also hitting home were Jimmy Webb, Burt Bacharach with Hal David, and Ray Davies from the Kinks, along with Jagger/Richards and Paul Simon. The idea was that for bands to have any sort of relevance, they had to write their own songs. This led to every band writing their own songs, often with mixed results, although cream always rises to the top and sediment the other way.

Lyrics aside, I knew the music component of songs entails melody and chords and either can be a starting point. Apparently, George Gershwin started his music with a chord structure, to which he added a melody line, while it seems Irving Berlin started with the melody line, to which he added the chords. Richard Rodgers would also have been melody first, as his melodies are far richer than the underlying chords. With Gershwin, the melodies are often quite simple, on top of a rich harmonic chord structure (*Summertime, I Got Rhythm, But Not For*

Me, How Long Has This Been Going On, I Got Plenty Of Nothin').

I've always been fascinated by interesting chord structures. That's one reason I admire the Beatles so much, as well as the Band and Brian Wilson. And why I regard George Gershwin as the greatest composer of the 20th century and *Summertime* as his greatest song. I would recommend the Ella Fitzgerald and Louis Armstrong version from the 1958 album 'Porgy and Bess' with a lush orchestral backing as my favourite example of music expression outside of the Allegretto movement from Beethoven's 7th Symphony.

To my ears, in the Beatles, John Lennon was a chord-first writer, while Paul McCartney was melody-first. Quite a few Lennon melodies hit just one note repeatedly, over changing chords (*Help, I'm Only Sleeping, Lucy In The Sky, Julia*) while McCartney has said that the melody of *Yesterday* just came to him one night and the following morning he got up to work out the chords on a piano. *Eleanor Rigby* and *She's Leaving Home*, I'd imagine, would have happened the same way. And of course there are times when the right melody and chords can just happen together. This is the realm of magic.

As for me, I've always been a chord-first writer, who then has to work hard getting a melody to fit nicely. This becomes more complicated when trying to come up with music for pre-written lyrics, my usual modus operandi. This can involve some editing of those lyrics to get everything to blend in a musical way and is usually met with good grace by those lyricists involved.

As a body of work, I think the Beatles are unbeatable for 60's music but for that decade's greatest song, it is hard to go past *God Only Knows* composed by Brian Wilson with lyrics by Tony Asher. The lyrics are lovely, as is Carl Wilson's angelic vocal and Brian Wilson's majestic arrangement, expertly played by the Wrecking Crew. But it is the ever-changing melody, ascending and descending at the same time, and sumptuous chord structure, that place this song somewhere beyond magnificent. Paul McCartney regards this as the greatest song ever written and has always been a champion of the 'Pet Sounds' album. Such a call from Sir Paul is not to be taken lightly, and neither is Benny from ABBA's choice of *Martha My Dear* from the Beatles 'White Album' as the one song he'd wished he had written. As for the Beatles, my five favourite songs are ... *Strawberry Fields Forever, She's Leaving Home, Something, Penny Lane* and *Norwegian Wood*.

Actually I thought the Beatles could get away with anything. On one of their famous singles, *All You Need Is Love* b/w *Baby You're A Rich Man*, both songs feature singalong choruses mostly based on one repeated note.

Back in Glebe, a group of us school kids, boys and girls, caught the double-decker bus into the city (a very short trip!) to see 'A Hard Day's Night' at one of the many movie theatres in town. I forget which one, maybe The Lyceum.

Speaking of double-decker buses, back in those days most people smoked and so they went to the upper deck to experience their international passport to smoking pleasure while the lower deck was strictly non-smoking. A sensible arrangement. However, sense went out the window in single deck buses where about two thirds down the length of the bus there was a sign with two arrows. One arrow pointed towards the driver and said, 'No Smoking.' The other arrow pointed to the back and said 'Smoking' ... as if the cigarette smoke was really going to stop at the 'No Smoking' sign. On a crowded bus on a wet or cold day with the windows closed there was no escape for those wishing to avoid cigarette smoke. Actually, in those days I was usually down the back with my 39 cent pack of Marlboro contributing to the cigarette fog.

Hot on the heels of the Beatles came the Rolling Stones who stirred the senses in different directions. For people like me, Brian Jones playing bottleneck slide guitar on *Little Red Rooster* was our introduction to the blues. I had never heard a sound like that before. With a drummer like Charlie Watts, who apart from being a modern jazz disciple, was also at home with how those R&B drummers could swing a band with a relaxed shuffle backbeat. Guitarist Keith Richard was a firm and fierce exponent of Chuck Berry style guitar, and there was an enigmatic bass player like Bill Wyman   and a captivating singer/frontman in Mick Jagger,

My growing Beatles and Stones reference library helped with working things out on guitar.

so the Stones were real eye and ear openers. In fact, for many like me, our introduction to Chuck Berry was via the Beatles and the Stones. Classic American music was now being played by classic British bands who opened the doors to great black music styles for youngsters eager to learn.

So, while this was going on, my cheap acoustic guitar was now down to 3 strings (the bottom 3 strings, E , A and D). Unperturbed, I played what I could on them and even started writing songs and forming little bands with school friends and other acquaintances. One of them, Brian Donnellan had an F hole archtop guitar with the full six strings and could play all the first position chords on them. I was mightily impressed and thought to myself, I'll have to get one of these. So, it was for my 15th birthday in July 1967 that I got my first real guitar, a Jason semi-acoustic electric guitar. Brian and I then went and got little 5 watt valve guitar amps with two knobs - one for volume and one for tone. And when it comes down to it, that's really all you need. Mine was a Goldentone and Brian's was a Vadis. We were now getting close to a real band. I remember Myron, our bass player, had a solid body bass but no amp. That didn't really matter as he couldn't play anyway but pretended very well.

Well, now that I had a guitar with six strings on it, I had a lot of figuring out to do. Brian could help a bit with his knowledge of 1st position chords with their open strings but I noticed that on those rare TV clips of the Beatles and Stones, they rarely played chords there. Instead, they were moving mostly up and down the guitar neck with what I soon learnt were barre chords. I therefore studied photos from the *Beatles Monthly Book* and the *Rolling Stones Monthly Book* that showed John, George, Keith and Brian playing these mysterious shapes. I then tried to line these chord shapes up with what I was hearing on their records.

This was a long process but I was determined, and not having a teacher, I probably took the long way around but eventually worked it out and ended up with a self-taught but solid knowledge of the fret board at least chordally. I could now do all the Chuck Berry variations and this in turn led to my own variations based on these barre chords, with the little finger doing extensions. Strongly rhythmic and groove-infused this style was, physically demanding but bound to drive along any rock and roll band. My own discoveries were a great source of joy and pride and I was happy to keep stumbling on to them without formal lessons as this helped sharpen the ear and feed the imagination which is the aim and destination of music.

Also from the 60's, I would add Dylan's *Like A Rolling Stone*, Paul Simon's *Bridge Over Troubled Water*, Ray Davies *Waterloo Sunset* and Jimmy Webb's *Wichita Lineman*. To this list you could add *Jumpin' Jack Flash* by the Stones, but that is as much about the band as it is about the song. The same could be said about the 60's recordings of Otis Redding, Aretha Franklin, Dionne Warwick, the Four Tops, the Fifth Dimension and others from that marvellous decade of music. How fortunate people of my age were to have grown up in the swinging 60's when great songs were a weekly, regular occurrence.

In the 70's, that number of great songs began to dwindle somewhat and in the decades since, great songs (and I mean great, not just very good) stand out like lone mountain tops, sparsely dotting an endless floodplain. It is telling that, while not in their highest category, one of the few memorable songs of recent times is the Beatles final song *Now And Then*. But then I would say that.

And now I'm going to blow any sense of cool out of the water. I first played guitar in public around 1967/1968 at so-called Folk Masses (the Catholic Church's attempt to embrace the modern). At my first one of these I came across a B7 chord in the accompaniment and I only knew, through my own Beatles and Stones studies, the barre chord shape on the 7th fret. Therefore, an old nun, leading the ensemble, showed me the 1st position chord fingering. So, there goes my rock and roll street cred. I was perilously close to Kumbaya-ville. But the magnetic pull of the Beatles and the Stones would prove too strong and planetary collisions were avoided. The music universe is indeed a strange place.

The early folk music style of Simon and Garfunkel also caught my ear. It was not exactly earnest, like previous folk music styles, and was not really religious, like *Kumbaya*, but had the same gentleness and melodic appeal. I've always thought of Paul Simon, with his songwriting, as a major figure and when I first heard their music, it was at a slightly older fellow's place in Glebe where he had a stick of incense burning and posters on the wall. Now, in mid-60's Glebe, this was all something quite new and different.

The times were changing, of course; not just Glebe, but everywhere. However, Glebe, being very close to Sydney University, began seeing an influx ... at first a trickle, and later substantial, of university students, bringing in new bohemian ideas to the staid old working class suburb.

From 1968 to the end of 1970 also saw new major music influences for me ... Jimi Hendrix, Eric Clapton (Bluesbreakers and Cream), Bob Dylan, Creedence Clearwater Revival, Led Zeppelin and Crosby, Stills, Nash and Young. I'll also admit to enjoying the relatively straight music (compared to the times) of Herb Alpert's Tijuana Brass, the Fifth Dimension and the pop records of Dean Martin and Andy Williams. Eclecticism was never a worry for me.

I remember one afternoon, listening to records. They were, in order, Howlin' Wolf, Bob Dylan and Herb Alpert's Tijuana Brass. Silly me! It never occurred to me that enjoying one style of music might automatically preclude some others. I still suffer from this 'problem' today.

In 1970, I was blown away when I heard 'The Brown Album' by the Band. This was ensemble music, vocally and instrumentally, of stunning originality unlike anything else at that time. It had the same effect on me as when I first heard the Beatles and, in time, The Band moved into 2nd place after them in my all-time favourite list, relegating the Stones to 3rd place. My holy trinity. It was bass player John Blake, then living in Glebe, a highly credentialed musician from some famous bands like Max Merrit and the Meteors and Levi Smith's Clefs among others, who first played me this stunning album. He was also in Tully, a legendary band who played in the Sydney production of 'Hair'. John played bass in our local amateur version of Hair at St. James Hall in Glebe. He was the only professional among us young amateurs in the band. I also remember that one or two of the male cast members enthusiastically participated in the famous nude scene but none of the girls did, to my disappointment.

During this time, I also played in a fairly amateurish rock band at some church social dances at the St. James Hall, with my old Catholic school teenage friends dancing away. My amp was updated to a 40 watt valve Fi-Sonic piggyback amp. Most of my learning process then was trying to figure out Eric Clapton's incredible playing. Jimi Hendrix was beyond me for a couple of reasons. First, his volume mastery of feedback and impossible sounds were out of reach for me as his guitar setup, with much lighter strings, could not be duplicated on my hard-to-play Jason guitar. It was only later that I learnt that Hendrix often tuned his guitar down to Eb, one semitone below standard guitar tuning. No wonder I found it hard playing along with him. That said, I eventually, many years later, mastered *Hey Joe* and *The Wind Cries Mary,* my two Hendrix favourites.

Eric Clapton, meanwhile, played in standard tuning, making it easier to play along with *Hideaway* in E, *Crossroads* in A and *Sunshine of Your Love* in D. So, while both guitarists were great, Clapton was accessible, while Hendrix was mysterious.

I had bailed out of school two weeks into the 1969 first term, age 16 and, with former school friends, Effie Cauchi and Bruce Wotton, was working as a clerk with Sydney County Council, treading time and not really knowing what was going to happen.

I was also friends with Mary Jurd whose older brother Mick Jurd was a well-established guitarist in the Sydney rock music scene, playing with the Levi Smith's Clefs. One day he showed me a progression of 3 jazz chords which led to future developments for me and which I still play today. Around this time, sweet soul music was also hitting home with me, and fellow, slightly older, beer drinking pals, Gary Stone and Sam Cauchi. For a while we were 'sharpies,' in dress only; Banlon t-shirts, high-waisted pants and short hair. Just a teenage fashion statement which was quite at odds with my musical influences and burgeoning hippie ideals, which were also quite at odds with my prior good-Catholic-boy background. And I was no fighter. Glebe was all I knew, but the world of music was calling.

A Glebe corner shop in 1955.

A TALE OF TWO BANDS
The Journey Begins...

TWO GUITARS
WITH BOB McGOWAN

Bands come in all shapes and sizes with different instrumental lineups. One of the basic lineups of the rock and roll era and a favourite of mine is two guitars, bass and drums. There were two approaches to this basic setup. Firstly, bands like the Shadows and Creedence Clearwater Revival featured a dedicated lead guitarist who played all the melodies and solos while the second guitar strummed a straight-ahead rhythm, very much in a subordinate role. This approach never varied and while standard procedure was somewhat predictable, although it remained their signature sound.

The second approach was favoured by bands like the Beatles and the Stones and featured far more interesting interplay between the two guitars. At times, the rhythm guitar could play a more funky part than the designated lead guitar and both guitars were likely to swap roles occasionally, resulting in more variety and interaction.

In both the Original Battersea Heroes and Uncle Bob's Band this is how Bob McGowan and I approached our two-guitar setup and although it was only a five-and-a-half-year period in the 1970's for us, in both bands this partnership remained a lifelong bond between us whenever we would get together. In this setup, I was the player in charge of the nuts and bolts construction, while Bob was the free spirit, adding unexpected layers to the architecture. This means I was the more disciplined player, better suited to providing a solid bedrock, while Bob was free to improvise. If the improvising didn't quite work, the basic feel and groove would still be happening. But, if the improvising did work, then creativity was afoot. And, of course, with inspired improvising, it can only happen once. Let's see what happens next time.

The last time Bob and I played together was one October night in 2017, one year before Bob died and this special, comfortable feeling was still there. A feeling unique in my experience of playing music.

Cook Road, Centennial Park 1972. Bob McGowan and I working on Django Rock.

VERSE ...

THE ORIGINAL BATTERSEA
HEROES

In January 1971, age eighteen-and-a-half, I joined my first professional rock and roll band, The Original Battersea Heroes. I was a green and enthusiastic amateur used to playing at church social dances and parties, and this was a big step up for me.

I had met Terry Darmody, singer with the Batterseas, at some of these church socials in Glebe and he asked me to fill in for Bob McGowan at a private party in Balmain, as Bob was away for that weekend. That's where I met bass player, Pete Nehill, and drummer, Dennis Burke, and Pete passed me this odd-looking cigarette with funny green stuff inside. Anyway, the music went well and the others were impressed and decided that since I had a solid but different guitar style to Bob, the two guitars would work well together as Bob was more of a soloist, while I worked more closely with the bass and drummer.

So, the Heroes became a quintet. Shortly afterwards, we had our first full band rehearsal and Bob arrived fashionably late with his wife, Kathy James. Bob was friendly and easy going but kept an eye on this young, green, upstart, joining him on guitar. For my part, I could hardly avert my gaze from Kathy, with her long blonde hair and very short miniskirt. Coming from Glebe, I had never seen any young woman like her. Certainly, miniskirts were short everywhere. Fashion of the day. But Kathy didn't seem to be following fashion. She had a bohemian air and confidence about her that was striking. Full of experience and individuality.

From the start Bob was the lead guitar and soloist and I was the rhythm guitar. I knew full well that I could play driving and inventive Chuck Berry and Keith Richard style rhythm and I also knew full well that I was no match for Bob's tearaway soloing. In fact, no one was. Whereas I based my style on others, Bob played like no one else. Pete Nehill had a stage name for Bob, 'Dazzling J Virtuosity!' But Bob was different to many flashy virtuosos on guitar who sometimes liked to demonstrate that they knew where every single note on every single fret on every single string was. No, Bob would often just hit the same note relentlessly, building tension, excitement and otherworldliness to the music. He really was like no one else.

The Batterseas also played with a much lighter feel, amplification notwithstanding, than other rock bands at that time due to originally being a jug band, where Dennis played washboard and Pete played tea-chest string bass.

OBH at Mittagong Pop Festival April 1971. I am nervously playing my Jason electric guitar having never played on such a big stage before. Note the subtle use of festival amplification.

THE ARTS FACTORY (1971)

The Original Battersea Heroes played quite regularly at the Arts Factory located at the southern fringe of the city. It was a venue that was 'hippie central,' full of incense, candles and tie-dyed clothes stalls, macrobiotic food with not a hamburger in sight, intoxicating fruit juices and hashish air, with a lot of good bands playing to out-of-it bean bag recliners and in front of a liquid light show backdrop. There were always a couple of bands on each time and I was particularly knocked out watching The La De Das, Company Caine, Sun with the young Renee Geyer, Greg Quill's Country Radio, The Flying Circus and Sirius, a bunch of Hungarian refugees playing an intense modern jazz/Zappa fusion-type music. I had never seen any band with such intense looks on their faces when they played. Terry nicknamed them 'Serious.'

Needless to say, the Battersea Heroes rock and roll had toes twitching, and any dancing that ensued was decidedly spaced out. Nimbin in the big city. Magic mushrooms in the concrete. Lucy wearing diamonds in the sky, and beads, beads everywhere. Still, this was a friendly and groovy place, quite safe, with no fights or 'agro,' just blissed out 'Dig It Man.'

In mid-1971 Bob, his wife Kathy and baby daughter Jessica, Pete and his girlfriend Christine, Terry and me all moved into a shared three-storey terrace in Paddington where my much older band mates introduced me to a wide range of early music styles, from jazz and blues to country and jugband. Many doors were opened, with Pete Nehill, in particular, taking me under his wing and furthering my musical education. Most importantly, this meant Louis Armstrong's revolutionary Hot Five and Hot Seven recordings from the 1920's, along with early jazz, black, white and creole. And, later on, it meant the symphonies of Beethoven and the modern jazz of Charles Mingus.

From Terry, I got Fats Waller and early jug band music, and from Bob, Doc Watson and early acoustic blues guitar styles. Chuck Berry was the idol for all of us and by that stage the Beatles had faded somewhat, but the Stones and The Band remained supreme and essential. As a green 19-year-old, not very hip or very good with girls, I was entranced with Kathy and Christine, both a few years older than me and both very beautiful. I also looked up to Pete Nehill, even dressing like him with Levi jeans, jean jacket and cowboy boots. He was an inspiring teacher, an authority and a role model. Along with Terry Darmody and mutual friend, Dom O'Donnell, I regarded Pete Nehill as an older brother.

Later that year, September 1971, the Heroes recorded an album for independent record producer Martin Erdman ... a Rock and Roll dance record which included five of our original songs. Guest musicians on the album were Tony Buchanan on tenor sax and the great Col Nolan on piano. Tony had a stellar career, playing with everyone from Col Joye and the Joye Boys to Renee Geyer, Crossfire and the Daly-Wilson Big Band; plus countless sessions with the great Col Nolan, pianist and organist extraordinaire, playing everything from rock and roll, to jazz, to television work.

It was a lively record and scored some favourable reviews but sounded a bit thin due to the bass being mixed very low, and sometimes not there at all, which was pretty strange as the rest of Martin Erdman's excellent recordings around that time sounded good and full. I can only presume that some sort of technical mishap must have occurred.

I play lead guitar on one song, *Ready Teddy*, but for the rest of the album, it's Bob blasting away with some incredibly exciting solos.

This album features Bob at his Battersea Heroes best and for that reason alone holds up well, and even with its faults can withstand the odd disparaging comment.

The reviewer, Gil Wahlquist, who wrote for the 'Sydney Morning Herald' and the 'Sun Herald', thought *Little Miss Lucy* was an outstanding evocation of the past. He found Bob's guitar outstanding and Terry's vocals 'a hoot!' Another reviewer saw flaws in the thinness of the recording but still thought it was a whole lot of fun. The friends who heard him playing it wanted more. In 2010 Martin Erdman re-issued the album on CD on his Du Monde record label bringing the Original Battersea Heroes into the modern digital age.

1972 was the year that Bob and I really got our double guitar act together. We were all living together at Cook Road, Centennial Park, and we had a new bass player, Bob Dames, as Pete and Christine were heading off to London. Sitting in the Cook Road lounge room, endlessly playing guitars and listening to records, a new music style was going to join the rock and roll of the Battersea Heroes. It was 1930's swing, specifically Django Reinhardt and Fats Waller which was intrinsically happy music and therefore a good fit with rock and roll.

Also, Bob, Terry and I got into the country blues of Ry Cooder and the songs of Randy Newman and were often joined by Kathy's brother, Steve James, who excelled at the slide guitar style of Fred McDowell. There were also times with the two guitars where I would just stop playing and listen to Bob do his acoustic finger-picking style, a mixture of Doc Watson, Merle Travis, John Fahey and Mississippi John Hurt. (In 2013 Bob released a CD, 'Live at Pure Pop', which just sounds like Bob playing at Cook Road, even playing a lot of the same songs).

So, for Bob, Terry and me, a musical melting pot was taking shape, an approach not geared towards fame and stardom nor towards any purist principles. Roots music? Yes, but the forest was pretty big. While Bob remained the go-to man for rock and roll guitar solos, we ended up swapping roles with the Django and Fats swing.

For this new style, I was often the lead player as I delved quite deep into the melodic Django style, but as usual Bob and I could swap lead and rhythm roles as we felt.

Bob and I only ever wrote two songs together and both were written one afternoon at Cook Road in early 1972. *One Fine Morning* and I*ntergalactic Space Age Girl* became staples with the Heroes and, later, Uncle Bob's Band. Also, at Cook Road, two other songs that became features with both bands were written, my *Rockin' Round The Bend* and *Church Song*, co-written with Terry. But for the most part, the Heroes remained a rock band playing covers, with Bob playing Lead and me playing Rhythm.

Terry was the lead singer/frontman and terrific harmonica player, Dennis remained on drums and during 1972 we had a few bass players, Bob Dames, John Blake, Trevor Wilson and Peter Knox. But the two-guitar setup was the driving force of the Original Battersea Heroes until the band started to fall apart in early 1973.

I ended up leaving and briefly joined the 69'ers. Bob also left and Terry put together a new band called The Heroes. Later that year, I started hanging out with Bob and Kathy again, rekindling our close personal relationship. This hanging out resulted in me missing a couple of 69'ers gigs and their booting me out which, no doubt, was mutually beneficial, and Bob and I put together a four-piece band to play a two-week residency at the Sawtell RSL club on the north coast of NSW. It took us a while to adjust to the requirements of RSL club music but the joy of playing with Bob again pointed to the future.

The McGowans were rather special. Bob and I had our unique bond, a brotherhood of guitars and bush walks, Kathy and I became very close with Bob's blessing, and I was always Uncle Tony to young Jessica.

The Three Amigos - Bob , me and Terry at Cook road 1972. Trying to work out this Django stuff could sometimes result in dumbfounded looks all round.

Uncle Bob's Band Dural 1974 *Adventures in Paradise* ... (left to right) Tony, Warwick, Keith, Terry, John and Bob.

CHORUS ...

UNCLE BOB'S BAND

That future for the two guitars came shortly after our RSL Club gig when I rang Bob and said 'Hey, let's put a band together.' He told me about a drummer from Glenorie that he was jamming with, along with a writer/lyricist, and suggested I came along. So, in January 1974, I jammed with Bob and Warwick Kennington whose drumming knocked me out. The jam went pretty well and soon we were joined by bass player/artist, John Taylor, who was one of two bass players we auditioned but got the gig, as he could do in-house posters and handbills. He was also a suitable madcap type to fit in with us and a good solid player, and then Terry came back on board as singer/frontman.

A few months later, Keith Shadwick joined on tenor sax and flute. This was Uncle Bob's Band. In its first incarnation as a quartet, two guitars, bass and drums with me singing, then a quintet with Terry singing, UBB was very much in the country rock style influenced by the Band and the Grateful Dead. This began to change when Keith joined with his modern jazz tenor sax style. Bob, Terry and I revisited our happy Django/Fats Waller swing of the Heroes days. Drummer Warwick and bassist John T. were unfamiliar with this style of music but happily succumbed to its charms.

An equally important element of UBB, which started pretty much straight away, was the emphasis on writing original songs fuelled by superb song lyrics (usually with music added later) by writer/ poet Mark Butler, soon joined by fellow writer, John Dease, with both becoming part of the band while never actually playing in it. Influenced by Dylan, Robbie Robertson and Robert Hunter (songwriter/lyricist for the Grateful Dead) they could be philosophical, *Going Home* and *Plainsong*, or narrative, *Quietly On The Run* and *Rosie*. Either way, this was a rich vein to mine and their words were put to music. All eight of us would meet, roll joints and try and work out how to get anywhere in the music game, or at least how to get out the front door.

Butler and Dease became our highly literate road crew, although neither could drive, but convention was never part of the UBB setup. They were equally a part of our philosophical agenda. Also, in those days, bands usually did their own carting gear around and setting up. The biggest bands had dedicated pros with an out-front sound mixer, side of stage fold back sound mixer and out-front lighting mixer. Hard working roadies all of them.

These songs also led to a new development in the two-guitar story. Firstly, as I wrote most of this music I concentrated on playing the chords and the feel of the songs along with the increasingly brilliant rhythm section of Warwick and John T. (as fine a rhythm section as I've ever played with before or since). More often than not Terry was out front singing these words with a signature quirkiness and charm while continuing his highly individual harmonica style, while Keith provided a rich palette of musical colours on tenor and flute.

However, we often added a new element to these songs and arrangements and this was, somewhere in the middle of the song, the Bob show. This was often an extended guitar solo that told its own story, at times a song within a song. Bob was given unlimited bars and free rein and never disappointed. Ex-Battersea Heroes, Bob, Terry and I had acquired a new sophistication and eloquence with these songs and our fondness for them never diminished.

Looming large in the UBB legend was our notorious 'Adventures In Paradise' shows, first at Dural Memorial Hall and then at Paddington Town Hall. At Dural, the view from the stage was incredible, with people dancing and romping about with unbridled joy, while on stage, we were joined by Kathy James, Kate Kennington and Margaret Bergman; exquisite hula dancers, adding a touch of glamour. The band/bands were fuelled by 'weed' and rum while the sense of oneness … stage and dance floor, band and audience, was palpable. No separation. No exclusion. Frankly, I've experienced nothing like it ever since.

These shows have already been well described by Terry Darmody in the liner notes/booklet for 'Django Rock' and also in an article from *Tracks* magazine back in 1974 by a marvellous writer, Annie Burton, which was probably the best article ever written on Uncle Bob's Band. Suffice it to say that 'Adventures In Paradise' sums up UBB better than anything else we did and those who saw either show probably never saw anything else quite like it, at least in terms of audacity, when there were numerous bands on the bill … all of them us in various guises, styles and costumes. And the posters for both the Dural and Paddo 'Adventures In Paradise' shows became collectors' items.

Meanwhile, swing was also the thing. With the arrival of Keith's jazzy tenor sax, the door to Django swing was reopened. While this style was originally played by the Battersea Heroes, it was Uncle Bob's Band who really pioneered the concept of a rock band playing swing jazz … Django Rock … But UBB was never a jazz band.

In the 1970's jazz bands were basically divided into two camps, the 'traddies' and the modernists. The modernists usually looked down their noses at the 'traddies' while the 'traddies' thought the modernists were up themselves, although both camps became more flexible over time. There was also jazz rock which included bands like Sun, Sirius, Crossfire and MacKenzie Theory, who could have a rock feel combined with a modern, complex form of jazz, mixed with some Zappa and Mahavishnu moments. This style was not really conducive to dancing, while 1930's swing was. With Django swing, it was my guitar that came to the fore. On these swing numbers, my solos were Djangoesque while Keith's tenor had a more modern, John Coltrane approach. We combined well and wrote a couple of instrumentals for the band, notably

Bobbin' Along which UBB recorded twice, with Keith soloing on flute, me playing Django lead on the bridge and Bob playing a tearaway rock guitar solo.

Here was Django Rock, or rock that beat with Django swing. Terry sang these swing numbers in a dapper style and sometimes Bob unleashed a scat vocal which would defy the laws of music and physics. Writer/musician, Alistair Jones, who joined in with the band on occasion, coined the moniker 'Gyro Gearloose' on a bumpy day for Bob's scat singing, in an article he wrote about the band for *Rolling Stone* in 1974.

At times UBB could also, courtesy of Keith and Bob, engage in a form of polyphony, 1920's New Orleans style. They could both solo simultaneously, each taking off on a free form trajectory where Keith could indulge in some of his avant-garde leanings while Bob went to the far reaches of his expanding universe. The rest of us in the band could only look on with admiration. These moments were as likely to happen in country rock originals like *Fly Away* or in our Latin-Australian flavoured *Brazil*.

So, while I was the Django specialist in the band, I suppose Bob was the true gypsy and Keith the true contemporary. I'll also point out that Keith played most of these songs in sharp keys as opposed to flat keys usually preferred by jazz horn players 'trad' and modern alike.

By now, it should be apparent that UBB had, apart from its other qualities, three highly distinctive soloists in its ranks. Quite a luxury. But we never had a hit record or indeed any recordings commercially released during our three years together 1974–1976. We thought we had a possible hit single with a song we recorded called *Chatswood* written by the two Johns, Dease and Taylor, but not having a record company behind us, nothing came of it. This was probably due to UBB's determination to do its own thing and sort of thumb its nose at the music industry as such. Not surprisingly the music industry, as such, did the same. We were an 'Indie' band long before that term became fashionable or in fact doable. Two exceptions to this stand-off were radio station 2JJ and, somewhat bewilderingly, television station, channel 10 (but that's another story).

However, 2JJ, located in the appropriately named Clapton Place Darlinghurst, was an important part of the UBB story before we moved to Melbourne in May 1976. In the two-and-a-half years prior to this we played a few live to air radio broadcasts in their studio to a live audience, which no doubt helped with our Sydney profile. 2JJ's Chris Winter introduced us once as 'a right bunch of ratbags,' a description we fondly held on to.

But UBB did record an album produced, 'on spec,' by Dave Flett, which was never mixed or completed, and some live studio recordings, all done late 1976, as well as two reunion albums; 'Unfinished Business,' recorded in 2004, and 'Now and Then,' in 2018, which was Bob's tribute album, after his death that year. It was entirely coincidental that the Fab Four's last ever song was also called 'Now and Then.' As John Dease recently joked to me, 'Some upstart band pinched our title!'

The two reunion albums were both largely made possible by the efforts and fundraising of Mark Butler, although I ended up contributing a quarter of the finances needed for 'Unfinished Business', while Butler contributed three-quarters of the overall cost. UBB bassist and resident artist, John Taylor, did the artwork for both, with liner notes by John Dease.

We called in some outside musicians to fill out the arrangements on keyboards and horns. Special mention to Ben Jones, who contributed a suave tenor sax solo on *Rosie,* co-written with John Dease and Nigel Harris, who played some Neapolitan accordion for *Music Lover From Way Back,* written by Warwick Kennington and Mark Butler. Nigel, along with Geoff Power, played the Tijuana Brass parts that I arranged.

For 'Now and Then,' Butler set up and oversaw a GoFundMe page which raised nearly $10,000. A great achievement. I, for one, didn't think it was possible but happily I was proved wrong and recording sessions were booked in Melbourne and Sydney to give Bob a proper send-off.

One song on this album, *A Very Chaste Affair*, another Butler/Burkys song, features one of my best horn arrangements for two clarinets, inspired by George Martin's horn charts for some Beatles songs. And it features another splendid vocal from Warwick as well as string bass from Ignatz RatskyWatsky (then visiting from Fox Trotsky). The bounce of the string bass was better suited to the song's strict dance band tempo rather than the otherwise excellent electric bass of John T.

The 1976 recordings featured the original six-piece band and these in-house recordings have now been commercially released in a two CD set, 'Django Rock'. These amply demonstrate the band's irrepressible danceability and include possibly the quintessential UBB song *Ragtime*, which, apart from my input as writer, vocalist and lead guitar, has the entire ensemble reaching rarified heights of excitement, as well as a thrilling tenor sax solo from Keith, with a couple of free-fall descents down to the lowest note on his sax, and highlighting Warwick's flamboyant drums and John T's rock solid bass.

This release also has, undoubtedly, the most successful UBB song ever - *Mr Domestic* - which has been commercially released three times in three different versions (not that Mark Butler or I have ever made any money out of it and, sadly, my new yacht will not be arriving tomorrow).

The first, in the late 70's was on a vinyl compilation album from Melbourne called 'Inner Sanctum' and came from the unfinished Dave Flett album and had a terrific and professional final mix from none other than Ross Wilson, Aussie Rock Royalty. Alistair Jones, a good friend of the band, joins in on piano and is prominent in this mix.

The second was the original rough mix from Dave Flett and was featured on a compilation CD album called 'Silver Roads' where UBB was in esteemed company. The third released version, and my favourite, is on 'Django Rock' and was a live in-the-studio recording. This very welcome release in 2022 was produced by publisher Tom Thompson and Ian Shadwick (Keith's brother) who also released a four CD set of Keith's prior band, Sun.

By the end of 1976, Uncle Bob's Band was finished and in 1978 Keith returned to the UK, becoming a notable author on matters musical. He died, prematurely, age 57, in 2008. As a side note, Keith and I were born on the same day, 24th July; Keith in 1951, me in 1952. Bob left us in 2018 age 73. However, we have the recordings to enjoy.

While generally well received in the spirit in which it was intended, the 2022 'Django Rock' release did result in some unexpected controversy with a, now former, colleague, leading to an unfortunate falling out between us ... oh well, there goes the Knighthood. But overwhelmingly, the response from band members, fans and friends to these live recordings from the original band in its prime, was firmly in the positive camp.

In this two CD set, the three principal soloists, Bob, Keith and I are all showcased equally, with the Django element finally seeing the light of day alongside our country rock and rock and roll forays while Keith's compositions, vocal and instrumental, were now rightfully recognised.

One song, *Dinah*, has all the distinctive UBB elements ... charming vocal from Terry, manic scat from Bob, laid back Swing/Rock in the slow section and groove when it picks up from Warwick and John; respectful melody in the verse, then hot tenor sax in the up-tempo from Keith, and my Django style has never been better recorded than on *Dinah* and *I'll See You In My Dreams*. While, elsewhere, Bob's peerless rock guitar solos blaze away in songs like *Soul City* and *Rockin' Round The Bend* and he blasts his rockets going to see the *Intergalactic Space Age Girl*. All of this was the real Uncle Bob's Band.

One final point on 'Django Rock' ... the cover photo featuring Uncle Bob with a welcoming smile and holding a guitar and a mandolin is just wonderful. I insisted on this photo being used instead of a more traditional group photo, and Tom and Ian readily agreed. It is very reminiscent of the cover of the Stones album 'Get your Ya Ya's out,' with Charlie Watts jumping and smiling and holding a couple of guitars. And, after all, we did name the band after Uncle Bob. This happened one day early on in 1974 at Warwick and Kate Kennington's house at

Forest Glen. After a rehearsal we were all sitting around listening to the Grateful Dead's song *Uncle John's Band* and trying to come up with a name. My recollection is that I suggested it but others may have at the same time. In any case, there was no argument. We were Uncle Bob's Band.

In retrospect, both OBH and UBB could be described as dance bands with a healthy sense of the ridiculous, imbued with *joie de vivre* and occasional pretension, but a genuine good time for all. And both stood out like pine trees in a polyester forest.

Uncle Bob's Band, 1975: (l to r) Bob McGowan, Keith Shadwick, unknown woman in front of Warwick Kennington, Terry Darmody, John Taylor and me.

My favourite Uncle Bob's Band posters, both designed by John Taylor.

UBB in action at a lunchtime university concert in 1976.

Margaret, me and mum, Sydney 1978-9.

CODA ...

SWANSONG

Getting back to that last time Bob and I played together at the Merton Hotel in Sydney, in October 2017; this was about one year after the Uncle Bob's Band reunion at the same venue. That gig in 2016 was an historic occasion with some great musical moments although a bit patchy as we had no rehearsal, just a quick talk-through an hour before playing, trying to recall old arrangements. As erstwhile musical director, I still managed to forget a few major ones though. The general consensus was that Warwick was the star of the evening which surprised no one and a good number of old UBB fans and friends came along and enjoyed the occasion, special as it was.

For the 2017 gig, neither Warwick nor John Taylor could make it, so Terry and I got a new bass player and drummer and rehearsed a bit with them. Bob would arrive just for the gig. No UBB originals were possible without the full UBB lineup, so Bob, Terry and I reverted back to our Original Battersea Heroes days and Chuck Berry was back on board.

While the year before at the UBB reunion, Bob, at times, seemed a bit overwhelmed playing with his old comrades again, this year he was firing on all cylinders, although the illness that would soon claim him was taking its toll. In an evening of highlights, one song in particular, Chuck Berry's *Nadine*, saw live music at its most exhilarating. The song just couldn't end. Terry would sing a rousing verse and chorus and then Bob would unleash a trademark solo. This pattern would repeat itself over and over and over, with no one wishing it to stop. Runaway musical momentum. The audience that night, sadly smaller than the previous year, were fortunate to witness something so remarkable ... the last joyful strains of the Original Battersea Heroes.

Over the years I've played with many greats but nothing and no one comes close to Terry and Bob when they're in this sort of mood ... no one.

In 2018, UBB decided to record our last reunion album as a few good quality songs had recently been written by its members and we wanted to feature Keith Shadwick via some recordings from our heyday in the 70's. However, time was running out for Uncle Bob with his deteriorating health. We recorded the new songs in Melbourne in November 2018, one month after Bob passed away. But he did manage to record a song co-written with lyricist John Dease in his final weeks. This was *Still Got Some Rambling To Do* and featured both his daughters, Eva (with Bob's second wife Annette), and Jessica (with Bob's first wife Kathy) - the Bobbettes, on backing vocals and Cousin Steve James on dobro.

This was Bob's finest composition and in a phone call to Bob a few days before he died, I told him so; also that he had set the bar pretty high for these new songs but we would do our best. Later Warwick added some tasty brushes work on drums and John Taylor added his usual impeccable bass line, making this a genuine UBB song. Due to a lack of finances, I was unable to travel to Melbourne for Bob's funeral but I was thankful that I had a last goodbye with him over the phone. I told him, on behalf of all of us in UBB, how much we loved him, asking him to hang in there for the upcoming recordings, although Dave Flett, who did a fine job as producer and who has also sadly left us, told me that Bob did not have long.

Two days before convening in Melbourne for the recordings, Dave phoned me to say he had found a rough demo tape he had recorded with Bob singing and playing guitar and suggested we try and include it in the new album. As general musical director of the band I immediately said yes, happy to include more of Bob. So, the four remain-

remaining members of UBB added our parts to Bob's vocal and guitar. Via headphones, we were recording with Bob in the studio. This song was *Right vs Right* and became our *Free As A Bird* (John Lennon's rough demo tape to which the three surviving Beatles added their parts). This was a fitting epitaph for Uncle Bob McGowan.

Happily, even though we are spread far and wide nowadays, I am still in contact with my fellow Bobbers, Terry Darmody, John Dease, Warwick Kennington and John Taylor. I feel no bitterness or regret with our lack of success, only happy to have stumbled through the journey with them. I suppose I am a glass half-full person but either way, half-full or half-empty, there is clearly room for more wine.

Soapbox Circus in action with music and acrobatics, 1977.

PRAM FACTORY & MATCHBOX

The Original Battersea Heroes and Uncle Bob's Band were all fans of Captain Matchbox Whoopee Band. They seemed like Melbourne soul brothers to us Sydneysiders and so it was inevitable that after UBB, I would hook up with the fabulous Conway brothers.

So in mid-1977, UBB was finished and so were the various lineups of the Whoopee Band. The Conways, with a bunch of new musicians, were now part of the Australian Performing Group (APG) based in Carlton, Melbourne at the Pram Factory. I was invited to join and jumped at the chance, so with a few clothes and my guitar, but no amp, I headed south on the 'Spirit of Progress,' or 'Spirit of Discomfort' as I called it.

Those at the Pram Factory called themselves The Collective and it was counterculture theatre writ large. Some were even driven to do their Chairman Mao exercises each morning. As the Conways and fellow Matchboxes were pretty wacky anyway, they fitted in well and I was happy to be a part of something completely different. And I learnt to juggle and walk around with someone standing on my shoulders.

This trick required a bit of upper body strength but, with a strong and straight back, wasn't too hard. For the climber, using the proper technique and approach was essential to get up there and then trust the support to hold on to the ankles and retain balance. I remember at one gig Pete Muhleisen and I were out in the beer tent and challenged all comers to emulate our circus trick. We did it first, me the support, and Pete the climber, and then watched numerous drunken and hapless contestants hit the deck and tables on their way down. Great fun!

This combination of musical satire, theatre, acrobatics and occasional lecturing was called the Soapbox Circus. We embarked on a tour from Melbourne all the way up to Cairns and back, and the APG decided to fund the next album by the band, now simply called Matchbox, as it differed from the Whoopee Band by being a bit more rocky and now playing at Melbourne's various rock venues. The funding was also helped by the band's appearance in an award winning television commercial for Jaffas. This album, called 'Slightly Troppo' and produced by Whoopee Band luminary, Dave Flett, was quite eclectic ranging from disco and punk sendups to Fats Waller, blues and originals.

Mic Conway and I came up with *Sleep* which we played on Countdown and I wrote the music to some Helen Garner lyrics in a song called *Home*, which is one of my all-time favourite collaborations. Helen had brought me her lyrics to *Home*, saying she thought I could add some sensitive music to them, as others she had collaborated with in the Melbourne rock scene, mainly just wanted to get their rocks off. I think I duly obliged.

With *Sleep*, Mic Conway had the lyrics and a basic melody for the verses but needed music for the chorus/middle 8 section. I provided the chords and harmonic structure for these verses and then proceeded to write a pretty good melody/chord structure for that chorus, ending with an Al Bowlly vocal triplet inflection that Mic was tickled by. The Matchbox Band worked out some nice vocal harmonies and we even included some Three Stooges-like sleep noises. All in all, a satisfying song.

Automaton, with lyrics by John Dease, had a Cha Cha Cha-type feel and was nicely arranged and played by the Matchbox Band, although I was never really convinced by the final mix on this. I thought it could have sounded a bit fuller; but it is definitely distinctive.

Later on, Matchbox played the original version of a song usually associated with Rob Luckey and The Works. This was *Button On A Shirt,* which I wrote with Mark Butler. Before it was new-waved by the

Works, the song had a Trini Lopez feel. Matchbox also had a go at *Ragtime* with Jim Conway's express train harmonica replacing Keith Shadwick's tenor sax.

Some of my favourite collaborations, apart from *Home* with Helen Garner, and *Sleep* with Mic Conway, are *That Smile* and *Rosie*, both with lyrics by John Dease, *Give Me Swing* with lyrics by Al Ward, *Eva* with lyrics by Carol Ruff and *Black Sheep* and *Going Home*, with lyrics by Mark Butler. Quite a talented and diverse bunch of lyricists. I've written some lyrics myself and some of them aren't bad but I'm more inclined to the music side so I'm more than happy to work with fellow creatives. This work, I might add, is always done separately.

Then there are Tone Poems - instrumental soundscapes about certain themes and moods, without words. These little descriptive pieces of music that I write are dear to my heart, still come to me from time to time, and are always a welcome visitation from the muse, daughter of Zeus and Mnemosyne. Actually there were nine muses, all sisters, presiding over poetry and song, among other things. Great bunch of gals! 'Slightly Troppo' also featured two arrangements by bass player Peter Muhleisen. These were full music notation charts for the Benny Goodman/Charlie Christian classic *Air Mail Special* and *Slumming* from the old Al Bowlly songbook, featuring lead vocal and three-part harmony. Jim Conway's harmonica, my guitar and Colin Stevens mandolin played the original big band parts along with Ric Ludbrook's tenor sax.

I had dim memories of music notation from my piano lessons many years previously, brushing up somewhat when I taught beginners guitar at the McGowan School Of Music. But, for the most part, my compositions and arrangements were not written down, just organised by ear as a lot of my fellow musicians in bands couldn't read music notation anyway.

These music charts by Peter Muhleisen really impressed me and were a definite challenge. And they inspired me to start writing music arrangements properly.

Meanwhile the two main vibes for me in Matchbox were two really strong lead vocalists in Mic Conway and Ric Ludbrook, and Jim Conway's exceptional harmonica playing. Not to mention living in vibrant and interesting inner-city Melbourne suburbs like Carlton, Brunswick and Prahran and the resulting attraction of vibrant and interesting women.

While at the Pram Factory, the Matchbox Band played musical and acting roles in a theatre production called 'Smack In The Dacks.' My role was that of a bartender and I had a few lines of dialogue to navigate. I must say my acting ability was and remains quite ordinary. However, on one occasion, after having a bit too much to drink, I delivered my lines with a certain amount of authentic, drunken conviction. I believe it's called method acting. On another occasion I overdid the method and missed the entire performance. For me, the show did not go on and I was mightily embarrassed. But my failings were minor compared to the later encroachment of a certain heroin brigade who were given their own time slot ...The Nightshift.

One of the more responsible members of The Collective, carpenter and general caretaker, Jon Koenig, even resorted to drilling holes in all the teaspoons so the heroin brigade couldn't do their thing. I remember, a few years earlier with UBB, I once accompanied our manager on a drive through Melbourne. I was not aware of things and we arrived at his dealer's place where he scored and shot up as I watched. He asked if I wanted any but I declined. Always hated needles! But my own stupidity included an 18-month bout with Tequila before I finally conceded defeat. It was too good for me and I haven't drunk it since. A sign of moderation is to accept defeat. Or, as Yoda would say, 'Failure, the greatest teacher is.'

The Matchbox Band and some APG members also linked up with some members of an actual circus troupe and together we held the first ever performance, under a big top, of Circus Oz. Years later, as part of the original performance, I received a small piece of the original big top circus tent. Who knows, might be worth something one day. Colin

Stevens left the band some time after this and was replaced by an extraordinary musician, Stephen Cooney, who played guitar, very groovy mandolin and didgeridoo!

In 1978, the Matchbox Band was featured in the movie version of the hit stage play 'Dimboola'. We played the band at the wedding reception. As a movie 'Dimboola' didn't quite work as it broke the first rule of comedy … it just wasn't very funny. It tried very hard to be funny and in fact was very serious about being funny which is probably why it wasn't despite good, solid performances from Bruce Spence and Bill Garner. For some reason, Stephen Cooney declined to be part of this endeavour. Prescient no doubt. A few months later he left and was replaced by a loveable Irishman, Louis McManus, who played guitar, mandolin and fiddle and who, with his English girlfriend Anna, hosted Irish parties at his house full of good 'craic.'

A further memory from filming 'Dimboola' was that Tim Robertson, who played a heavy-drinking Catholic priest, and I would often meet up at the ever-present beer keg to refill our glasses with the same greeting/justification … continuity!

Also in Melbourne with the Matchbox Band, I got my first Vox amp, a 1974 AC30 which had the sound of the Beatles all through it. I continued playing through this amp up to my time with Lonnie and the Leemen until bequeathing it to my son, Marc, when it just got too heavy for me to cart around. It remains the best sounding amp I ever had.

While in Matchbox, I started playing cricket, having previously played a bit as a youngster. I was a handy medium/fast bowler and a batsman who preferred hitting fours to defending with a straight bat. I also enjoyed fielding, being quite agile in the field and good at catching. For those who are unaware, catching an airborne hard cricket ball at pace, without proper technique, can be painful. Mic Conway was also a cricketer, a solid batsman and captain, of course, as was Michael Price from the APG at the Pram Factory.

I used to proudly say I played for the MCC – the Matchbox Cricket Club! A few years later, in Sydney, I played competition cricket mainly as a bowler and was once on a hat trick. The first ball swung back in from the 'off' and hit the middle stump. When the next batsman came in, I delivered the same ball, only better and faster, and knocked the middle stump out of the ground. What excitement! On a hat trick! The third ball went down 'the leg side' to the keeper. The batsman swished at it but missed. Immortality denied!

Meanwhile back with Matchbox …

I was alternating between Sydney and Melbourne in an on-again, off-again romance with Margaret Bergman, which began in 1975 in the UBB years, with Margaret being my first serious relationship, and when UBB moved to Melbourne in mid-1976, Margaret and her daughter Poppy came with me. Margaret also knitted me a Rasta hat, red, green, yellow and black, during my Bob Marley fixation years. In late 1979, I left Matchbox and moved back to Sydney to be with her and where it appeared I was, in a musical sense, a spent force at the age of 27. The punk/new wave movement held no interest for me. I was as irrelevant as the old school music styles I loved. There was only one thing to do … start from scratch and reinvent myself in jazz bands.

The Matchbox band outside the Circus Oz big top tent for its inaugural show: (l to r) Mic Conway, Rick Ludbrook, Gordon McLean, me, Colin Stevens, Jim Conway and Peter Muhleisen in 1978.

STARTING FROM SCRATCH

Starting from scratch in jazz bands meant just that. Whereas after a decade of playing in rock bands I had some sort of reputation, in jazz I was a nobody, a beginner. And in a strange twist that I cannot really explain, it ended up that I played better Django style guitar during the 1970's in rock bands than I ever did after that in proper jazz bands. Also, at this time, the relationship with Margaret finally ended. I went into jazz with the notion that it was mainly carried by horn players, brass and reed, and the guitar was really a support instrument. Of course, the chordal and harmonic sophistication of jazz really appealed to me and as I had a strong rhythmic style, that's what I did.

So in 1980 I joined my first jazz band, Swing 84, led by clarinettist and local Balmain personality Rod Lawless. Also on hand was fellow UBB member, Warwick Kennington, on drums and guitarist/ bassist Kim Cook. Kim and I would alternate sets on guitar and electric bass. Originally, the brilliant Tom Baker played tenor sax but soon Murray Hill (equally brilliant) joined with his alto sax.

The clarinet/sax sound was very pleasing and Swing 84 had a lengthy weekly gig at the West Ryde Hotel, always with a good crowd, people coming from all over. An amusing recollection is that Murray Hill, a fan of Charlie Parker, wanted us to do Parker's *Donna Lee,* based on the chords of the old standard *Indiana*. The head (melody) is continuous bebop lines, almost entirely triplets and quavers and it took me weeks of learning it from the sheet music until I could actually play it. However, when it came to the guitar solo, so scant was my bebop jazz improvising that I usually reverted back to Chuck Berry and blues' licks. This facet of mine was usually frowned upon in jazz circles, rightly so I suppose, but I never saw anything wrong with it, remaining as eclectic as ever and possibly fooling myself.

Also in 1980, at a Swing 84 gig at the London Hotel in Balmain, I met Linda Robertson. The following year we were married and very shortly afterwards our daughter, Amie, arrived. I was there at her birth at the Crown Street Women's Hospital Birthing Centre with midwives in charge. The most amazing experience of my life as I'm sure it was for both mother and daughter. I distinctly remember after the birth, walking through the hospital to find a phone to tell my mother that her granddaughter had arrived. I also distinctly remember my feet not touching the ground, elated as I was.

Three years later, our son Marc, arrived in similar fashion at the Paddington Women's Hospital Birthing Centre, again with midwives. Both hospitals have now been converted into apartments. A sad reflection, but both our children were born naturally and safely in a hospital and neither birth cost a cent, thanks to Medicare. And my two children remain my proudest achievement.

Warwick Kennington drumming for Uncle Bob's Band, 1975 (photo Ian Shadwick).

Balmain pub jazz circa 1982. Rod Lawless, clarinet, Paul Simpson, tenor sax, Jeff Percival, tea chest bass, Harvey Fisk and me on guitars. You could walk into many pubs in those days and see a rough and ready jazz band swinging away in the corner. It didn't just happen 'way on down south, London Town.'

1989. Tony with Linda and Pop, Amie and Marc in front.

BALANCING ACT - DAY JOB, FAMILY LIFE and MUSIC

The 1980's saw some changes ... with a wife and then two children to support, the vagaries of the music game were not really sufficient, so I started working a day-job to keep a roof over our heads. Not having any qualifications or skills apart from playing guitar, I started working as a delivery driver, which I continued, in various forms, until my knees made me retire at age 68. I think playing (oldies) competition soccer for many years didn't help them much either. At this game I had minimal ball skills, being a late starter, but I was a fast runner with the ball at my feet. In fact, up to the age of 60, even 62, I could outrun most of the other guys, all younger than me. But nowadays I'm so slow it takes me an hour-and-a-half to watch 60 Minutes!

So, early in 1981, when Linda was pregnant with Amie, who arrived that August, I started working for a laundry company, doing the city-run, delivering hand towels, tea towels and cotton pull-down towel dispensers. This ended up working out well for me as, while the hours were 7.30am-4pm, if you were quick and efficient with your run, you could go home early. I ended up finishing work usually between 1pm and 2pm, and so could then go home to the family life. This meant that for the years 1982 and 1983, I spent plenty of time with my baby daughter. Linda had Amie all to herself during the mornings and if I had a music job at night, Amie would be asleep anyway.

Shortly after Marc arrived in November 1984, I was promoted at work to take over as branch manager at the Russell Vale depot, just north of Wollongong. We moved down there, renting a house at nearby Corrimal. Again the hours were 7.30am-4pm and, as manager, I had to stay till 4pm. But this was an efficient little branch with no late finishes. Plus we lived five minutes away. I could even go home for lunch so again I could spend plenty of time with our new baby son.

Occasionally I had night-time music jobs in Sydney which involved late nights and a lot of driving but as branch manager I had the luxury of a company car which helped immensely. And travelling is 'par for the course' for a musician.

Linda was a stay-at-home mum and an excellent one at that and so Amie and Marc had happy and secure childhoods with a full-time mother to look after them and a father who was able to spend daytime hours with them.

Linda was so good at this that she ended up babysitting for some of our friends in Sydney and down south. She looked after Jim and Steph Trainer's daughter, Erin, for a while in Sydney and at Corrimal, Kate Gosford (formerly Kate Kennington) and Greg Pickhaver's (H.G. Nelson) son, Max.

Musically, during this time, I was acquiring a collection of jazz records compiled by the Institute of Jazz Studies at Rutgers University in America under director, Dan Morgenstern. This was a 25 box set, each containing four albums called 'The Greatest Jazz Recordings Of All Time' and was the Institute's official archive collection. This was distributed by the Franklin Mint Record Society and ended up being as impressive as it sounded, being a complete and enjoyable education for me. This was where I really learnt about jazz. I had great satisfaction in compiling different cassette tapes of my favourite tracks for fellow musicians like Geoff Power, Warwick Kennington and Dave Clayton. You gotta hear this!

In the late 1980's, after we had moved back to Sydney, Linda started a university course, as a mature age student, to become a teacher and later on, Amie followed in her footsteps when she finished school. Marc was like his father and didn't quite make it to the end of school although he lasted a year longer than I did. I suppose some of us are just unteachable and just have to work things out for themselves, and intelligence and imagination can exist with or without qualifications.

Meanwhile, Swing 84 underwent a startling metamorphosis into a country and western band called Boot Hill, with Murray Hill changing from Charlie Parker to Hank Williams. He carried both off with some aplomb. Rod Lawless was not part of this country band but he continued to lead a few different versions of Swing 84, playing mainly at the London Hotel and I played with him in a few of these lineups.

This was good Sydney pub jazz band music at a time when many pubs in Sydney had one. In fact, I can remember playing at virtually every pub in Balmain and Rozelle at this time. What a musically healthy and convivial time it was! The money was usually minimal but it really was a part of life for players and punters alike. High profile, star-posturing was not a part of this, just low key but swinging jazz music in a pub. Nowadays, it has been replaced by Foxtel sports channels. Your Honour, I rest my case.

In 1982 and 1983, a short-lived but very interesting band was formed ... Noises For The Talkies. I joined up again with the fabulous Conway brothers, Mic and Jim, now both living in Sydney. We were joined by two diverse but extremely talented musicians. Peter Deane-Butcher played jug, tea chest bass (and I mean actual notes in tune on the tea chest bass) as well as general lunacy that rivalled the great Mic Conway; and Gypsy Dave Smith, who played great acoustic blues guitar and even managed a face-slapping solo or two.

The band only played a few times and doesn't figure in the usual compilation of music events but remains high in my estimation and also in my daughter, Amie's, recollection of charming kid's songs like *Jollity Farm* and *Hunting Tigers In India*. From the age of one or two, Amie came along to many of my music gigs, night and day, with Linda making sure she had a comfy little bed under the table for late-night gigs; but mostly she was a night owl.

Music kept on. I drifted into trad jazz playing with clarinettist Wally Temple, cornetist Nat Oliver, and trumpeter Jiri Kripac. Then into the extended Dixieland gig empire of John Halgren who, with his agency contacts, seemed to have an endless supply of Dixieland trio gigs all over the place from shopping centres (including all the Westfield openings) to corporate gigs, office parties, weddings, functions and Christmas parties.

I even, dressed in ridiculous lederhosen at Oktoberfest, played in a couple of German bands, utterly devoid of Germans … dignity, always dignity.

Many fine musicians made up these various trios. Some people may look askance at these sort of bands but to be professional, many things were required to actually be paid, and expertise is always to be admired.

Eventually, the Swing Factory was formed to play at corporate gigs at function centres. This was an eight-piece band … 3 saxes, trumpet, trombone, guitar, bass and drums. Playing cut-down, big band charts, hardly a week went by without the Swing Factory playing one or two gigs.

The Swing Factory really whetted my appetite for big band playing with the swirling saxes, the biting horns and the swinging rhythm section. With good, professional players and good readers this was impressive music, even when playing old warhorses like *In the Mood*. At these corporate functions, people were always on the dance floor which made our obligatory dinner suits more palatable.

SWEET ATMOSPHERE

Sweet Atmosphere was a late 1980's to early 1990's Django/Stephane band and featured the great swinger on violin, George Washingmachine, and Ian Date, a true virtuoso on guitar. Natalie Morrison played double bass and I did the Joseph Reinhardt role on rhythm guitar.

This was superb acoustic music and we recorded an album of swinging Quintet type songs. My favourite recollection is that at one gig during a guitar solo, Ian broke a string (G or 3rd string) then almost immediately after, the D or 4th string broke. Now when something like this happens, normally the guitarist stops the song as soon as he can to put some new strings on. Not Ian. Not only did he continue playing the solo on just the top two strings, but the solo became an inspired piece of melodic and rhythmic invention and went on for a few more choruses. I was astounded and witnessing this from just a few feet away, it was a memorable musical moment. But I guess virtuosos can do this.

Another recollection is that I played at James Morrison's wedding with the Sweet Atmosphere lineup above. This was out on Sydney Harbour on board a classic 'olde world' sailing ship. Later on we played a bit at the reception at Don Burrow's Supper Club, then a high-end jazz venue. Later in the evening, James Morrison got up to play with some of his top-shelf jazz guys. As Sweet Atmosphere had just finished playing, I decided to remain on stage, playing quiet rhythm guitar with these jazz all-stars. The only time I ever played with James Morrison.

Apart from playing jazz in the 1980's, I also started two other important music collaborations with guitarist, singer/songwriter, Al Ward, and double bassist/arranger, Dave Clayton. Also in this mix was singer, harmonica and mandolin player and all round *bon vivant*, Al Meadows, as well as seriously good singer/blues guitarist, Jim Jarvis.

The Other Brothers and Duck Soup lineups both played a mixture of 1930's swing, country, blues, jug band and occasional Beatles, and were right up my alley … Eclectic Boulevarde.

Sweet Emma's was a New Orleans theme restaurant on Sydney's northern beaches; a delightful family-run business. For a few years, from 1986, I played a duo gig with clarinet player, Colin Beale, playing old style New Orleans Jazz. This was hard work for a guitar player but good practice in being a self-contained band (when the clarinet stopped, it was just you). Also the food, Cajun and Creole, was superb … the blackened Cajun style steaks forever etched in my memory along with the gumbo.

And so the 1980's continued with me working hard during the day and increasingly doing gigs with jazz bands, so much so that I had to keep reminding myself that I was, in fact, a self-taught rock and roller. Many jazz players back then had done the jazz course at the Conservatorium and were far ahead of me in schooling and qualifications and sight-reading ability.

In December 1989 came the first gig ever by a ten-piece big band, plus vocalist, which would become the greatest musical outfit I would ever be a part of. Originally called The Casablanca Roof Orchestra, but later changed to The Cafe Society Orchestra, this was some band.

THE CAFE SOCIETY ORCHESTRA

Geoff Embleton was the mastermind behind this marvellous band. He was also the singer, dapper frontman and conductor. One of his jokes was that as a young man, working in his hometown London, he was described as one of England's most promising young conductors ... he was working on double decker buses at the time. And he remains, along with Al Meadows, the most convincing wearer of a fez I've ever met. His vision for the band was simple but spot on. Most, if not all, big bands back then played standard big band charts ... Glen Miller, Dorsey Brothers, Artie Shaw and the like. These charts were often not original but stock, simplified versions that had minimal jazz content. They were however functional and dancers loved them.

Geoff decided he would up the jazz content and concentrate on early pre-swing Duke Ellington classics from the late 1920's and early 1930's. He tracked down some authentic Ellington charts as well as some astutely chosen pop song charts from that period which were replete with retro charm. To play these charts properly would require not only good section players but excellent jazz soloists. So Geoff rounded them up and eventually settled on a lineup that included, in my view, some national treasures from the Swing and mainstream jazz ranks. I hasten to add I was not one of them. I knew full well that I was there for my solid, swing rhythm guitar, in a Freddie Greene style, that would serve as an anchor for the stars.

So who were these stars? Drum roll please!

1991. The lineup of the Cafe Society Orchestra. Back row, (l to r) - Kenny Powell, piano - Freddie Donelato, trumpet - Eric Holroyd, trumpet - Dave Basden, tuba - Paul Williams, tenor sax - Len Barnard, drums. Seated, (l to r) - Geoff Power, trombone - Jim Elliot, alto sax - Geoff Embleton, bandleader - Ron Nairn, alto sax - and me.

Noises For The Talkies, 1982. The fabulous Conway brothers with Pete Deane-Butcher on jug and Gypsy Dave Smith and me on guitars.

First the national treasures.

Len Barnard on drums was one of the greatest drummers Australia has produced. Playing in the trad, swing and mainstream jazz styles, Len understood the concept of colours in jazz drumming better than just about anyone. For about 12 years at the Cafe Society's residency at the Unity Hall Hotel in Balmain, I sat about two feet away from Len Barnard's hi-hat. A highlight of my life.

Tom Baker, cornet. The incomparable, internationally renowned Tom Baker. A big, friendly man, American-born with a big, sumptuous tone. Tom played lead cornet and he was the boss. He was the same age as me and died overseas, tragically young at 49. Many people in many continents were shattered when this happened.

Bob Henderson, trumpet. While Tom Baker was lead cornet, Bob Henderson was the perfect foil on 2nd trumpet. Playing most of the solos, Bob had a different style, a more laid-back approach based on subtle phrasing that often reminded me of Bix Beiderbecke. Together, Baker and Henderson were the sound of The Cafe Society Orchestra.

Paul Furniss, 2nd Alto and clarinet. Nicknamed 'The Chief' because, well, he was. The Paul Furniss solos on clarinet, alto and occasionally soprano sax were frequently the highlight of the week. He remains one of Australia's greatest ever jazzmen.

Paul Williams, tenor sax and clarinet. What style, what tone, what swing! Effortlessly done. Born in England, he is my favourite tenor sax player and although he wasn't all that keen on his clarinet he could actually out-clarinet anybody.

Then there were the stars … The Cafe Society had two wonderful pianists. Firstly, Kenny Powell, who was also the house-pianist on the Morecombe and Wise Show in England during the 1960's. When he was with The Cafe Society I would often say that the band had four sections, the brass section, the sax section, the rhythm section and the Kenny Powell section. After a while, he was replaced by Chris Taperell, as solid, reliable and inventive as anyone and pretty much first choice piano player for any jazz band in Sydney. Such was the high regard he was held in.

The original bass instrument in the Cafe Society was tuba played by the enormously talented Dave Basden, who was also an accomplished arranger, writing many of the Midday Show Band arrangements. His charts for The Cafe Society were top shelf and a pleasure to play, my favourite being Summertime with original Gershwin orchestrations arranged for our ten-piece.

After he left, Chris Qua joined on double bass. 'Smedley' was a great bassist to work with, always comfortable, always swinging and he was much loved and fondly remembered by everyone.

The lead alto was Ron Nairn and he was a great section leader. The sax section of Ron and the two Pauls was frequently miraculous as they handled many intricate and challenging charts seemingly with ease. Nothing was beyond them. The lead alto role is often an unsung hero as pretty much all sax solos are played by the tenor and the 2nd alto but Ron Nairn's lead alto was the main section voice.

On trombone, and matching Tom Baker and Bob Henderson in perfect synchronicity, was Jim Elliot. An immensely talented multi-instrumentalist, 'Jimbo' would end up sitting in six different chairs in the band. He played trombone and when required 1st alto, 2nd alto, tenor, piano and even bass sax when double bass or tuba were not available. Formidable is hardly the word and when I got my first CD player and wanted to build up a classical music collection, 'Jimbo's' advice on classical selections was sought and acted on without hesitation.

Geoff Power played cornet and trombone, and while not in the original lineup, was always associated with the band, filling in for anyone in the brass section, and joining the band full time, after Tom's demise.

On guitar I hardly ever took a solo, just kept the rhythm going in the time-honoured big band tradition. But I had the best seat in the house. Not only was I a fan of the band, I was in it. However, I did have another string to my bow. The Cafe Society Orchestra played a couple of my original tunes/arrangements which I scored for the ten-piece band. The songs were *Jean Baptiste* (my tribute to Django) and *Recklessly* (co-written with Mark Butler lyrics but only ever played as an instrumental).

Looking back, quite possibly the proudest musical moments of my life were hearing the Cafe Society play this music of mine.

At one stage, I also wrote a little trio arrangement for the first part of the Allegretto (2nd) movement of Beethoven's 7th Symphony. I played the chords on the guitar, Paul Furniss played the melody on clarinet and Jim Elliot played a counter-line on bass clarinet. This was the A minor section, and many years later, during one of the COVID lockdowns, I got round to working out the remaining sections in A major (which was as hard as it sounds) and this became one of my guitar party pieces. Rarely played, but I did trot it out at Pete Nehill's wake in 2023, which was fitting as he introduced me to this supreme symphony in the first place.

For many years, The Cafe Society had a Tuesday night residency at the Unity Hall Hotel in Balmain, usually to packed crowds. One night, at the end of the first set, the crowd was so big there seemed no way I would get to the bar for a drink, so I went to another pub up the road for a beer. We played many other gigs and functions, memorably the Manly Jazz Festival and our crowning achievement, Jazz At The Domain, which was the premier, prestige jazz concert in Sydney, usually reserved for superstars like James Morrison and top of the charts jazz/pop singers, like Vince Jones and Grace Night.

Also, for a couple of years we played at the New South Wales Art Gallery Christmas party. This was for the friends of the Art Gallery who no doubt were sponsors and this was a thank-you event for them. It coincided with different exhibitions from European Masters so, in between sets, we could wander down to peruse these masterpieces in relatively quiet surroundings and with a glass of red wine. All very civilised. It was not hard at all to feel very comfortable with such highbrow working conditions.

An early version of the band is featured on a CD but, sadly, the classic lineup was never recorded properly, which remains a profound disappointment and Australian music's loss. At its peak, The Cafe Society Orchestra could have taken on any comparable outfit from America or Europe and comfortably held its own.

MUSIC WITH DAVE CLAYTON

When I spoke about the enduring bond I had with Uncle Bob McGowan, there is another musician of whom that could be said … bassist and arranger, Dave Clayton.

We began playing music together in the 1980's with Al Ward, Peter Deane-Butcher and Alan Meadows in The Hokum-On-Somble, a fun string/jug band. Dave and I were also the rhythm section, along with drummer Dennis Sutherland, in The Swing Factory, playing all those corporate functions at venues like the Convention Centre at Darling Harbour. While in The Cafe Society Orchestra, Dave Basden was responsible for most of the original charts; in The Swing Factory, it was Dave Clayton. To read, play and listen to quality charts gives a deep appreciation of how fine music works and is a feast for the musical imagination.

The writers of these charts – the arrangers – are the unsung heroes of the music world. With rare exceptions, such as Duke Ellington (also a composer) and Sir George Martin, known for his work with the Beatles, they are relatively unknown. But without them, music would be nowhere near as magnificent or memorable. The arrangers provide thoughtful musical notes and phrases for musicians to play when supporting a – famous or not – melody line. The composer combines lines of poetry and lyrics, with a hopefully memorable melody. Then, the arranger, with often an even greater musical skill, expands this simple melody into a stunning ensemble piece. Well may we say, Author! Author! Or Composer! Composer!. We should also say, Arranger! Arranger!

Dave and I also played in various jazz bands, usually 'trad' to mainstream and played on Geoff Power's first solo CD called 'Aspects Of Power.' Before deciding on this, Geoff asked us for suggestions for the album title. My suggestion was, of course, 'Sgt. Power's Lonely Hearts Club Band.' Also on this album were Paul Williams, Ed Wilson and drummers, Ian Bloxsom and Will Dower and it showcases Geoff's multi-instrumentalist talents.

We also put together a band called The DaveTones, usually a duo but when joined by a drummer, we put his name first, so it could be Bob and The DaveTones, or Merv and the DaveTones. For my sister, Dana's, 50th birthday we were joined by my son on drums, and so we were Marc and The DaveTones. Speaking of parties, from the age of 17, I've been to hundreds, always playing in a band at them. I therefore don't really know what to do when I go to one and don't play music. I really feel awkward and uncomfortable. Plus, I don't get paid.

The work of Dave Basden and Dave Clayton inspired me to write my own arrangements for horns, brass and reed, and rhythm. Two early examples are on Al Ward's 1997 solo album, 'Leaving The Island', featuring all original songs by Al, including two co-written with and arranged by me. This album was produced by Dave Clayton and Dave, Al Meadows, Dennis Sutherland and I, all play on it, along with the horn players from Swing Factory. I still listen to it from time to time and it's a delightful collection of songs from the witty and urbane Al Ward.

Al's album really got me thinking that I should record my own album of original songs. So, when I turned 50 in 2002, my wife Linda suggested to people that instead of presents they could perhaps contribute some money for the recording. My main lyricist/collaborator Mark Butler, jumped in with $500, as the album was going to feature mainly our co-written songs, as well as a couple of Django tributes I had written. Top of the Muso list for this record was Dave Clayton and some luminaries from the Cafe Society; Len Barnard, Chris Taperell, Paul Furniss, Ben Jones, Nigel Harris and Geoff Power.

On Geoff's 1999 album 'Aspects of Power', I had sung an original by Mark Butler and I called *Billie*, a song about the legendary jazz singer, Billie Holiday. I was going to do another version for my album but decided to get one of my favourite singers, Carol Ralph, to sing it. It became my favourite track on the album. *Jean Baptiste* (Django's real name) was another highlight with Paul Furniss on soprano sax and Nigel Harris on trumpet, playing the melody, and each playing wonderful solos. Nigel with an elegiac touch and Paul quite Django-like in its playfulness. The Cafe Society would often feature this arrangement as well.

Nigel also played accordion on the other Django tune I wrote called *Romany Remedy*. This was written back in 1975 and the title comes from a book my girlfriend Margaret had, about gypsy cure-all's. The album is called Heavy Mettle (title courtesy of Mark Butler) and was recorded, mixed and mastered, quite superbly I might add, by Ron Craig at his Delta Studio in Sydney. I was so proud to have my music played and recorded by such classy professionals.

In 2016, I decided to do a second album of original songs, which included a couple co-written with lyricist John Dease; *They Can't Hold A Candle To You* and *That Smile* which I've played in various jazz ensembles. He, Mark Butler and I had continued writing songs together after the Uncle Bob's Band days. For this album, Dave Clayton was back on double bass and Bob Gillespie played drums. Terry Darmody also sang and played harmonica and Lee Hutchins played some groovy, swinging tenor sax. There were no big band arrangements on this album, 'Meanwhile Back At The Boogie Farm,' but a lot more acoustic guitar playing, and featured engineer/producer, Marcus Holden, playing some nice fiddle on one of the tracks *Something Cute For Poppy*, one of four old UBB songs included in the album.

Dave Clayton and I continue to play together from time to time and just like with Uncle Bob McGowan, it is always the same comfortable musical feeling I have and enjoy. In a really nice symmetry, both Bob and I, and Dave and I, have played in fathers-and-sons lineups.

In a UBB reunion for Bob's 50th, Bob and I played guitars, while Bob's son Tal (with his second wife Annette) was on bass, and my son, Marc, was on drums. And playing at an office Christmas party, Dave played piano, I was on guitar, Dave's son, Sam, was on bass, and Marc was on drums. I might also add how proud I am that my daughter Amie learnt piano properly, completing the examinations of the Australian Music Examinations Board (AMEB). That she can play Chopin on the piano pleases me no end. Both Amie and Marc, like me, can thank Uncle Vlad.

Mid 1990's jazz quartet. Geoff Power, cornet - Paul Williams, tenor sax - Dave Clayton, double bass and me on guitar.

WEST RYDE
PRIMARY SCHOOL BAND

Amie and Marc went to West Ryde Public School and both were school captains in their final years. After one year's school presentation which had a less than inspired keyboard ensemble playing some dire piece I decided I would step in, donate my time and expertise, and organise a proper school band for West Ryde.

This continued for over 20 years featuring students from mainly years 5 and 6. The idea being that prior to going to High School, they would inspire some Year 3 and 4 budding musicians to join the band. This proved successful and after a while my donated time was replaced with the school organising a modest music fee for band members.

These little bands were a great joy with the range of instruments being piano, keyboards, flute, violin, glockenspiel, guitars, drums and recorders. And I wrote little arrangements of mainly groovy 60's songs which had them swinging. We often played Beatles songs, some classical things, Inspector Gadget, ABBA, Queen and one year we even had a go at *Live And Let Die* sans fireworks.

I have fond and proud memories of these bands and I hope all the kids involved in them came away with a further appreciation of music and how it works.

CROWLE HOME

For 10 years, 1997-2007, I was the music man at Crowle Home in Meadowbank, a private home for disabled institutionalised people. These were music therapy sessions and, apart from the obligatory *You Are My Sunshine* and the like, I had a rather extensive repertoire. Even so, I made a point of learning any personal favourites from any of the residents which only extended the repertoire and kept them all happy. This led to music from the Delltones, the Seekers, Rodgers and Hammerstein and Lerner and Loewe musicals. Delightful songs all, to go with my Elvis, Beatles and 60's pop. Despite their constant need for day-to-day help, music was a connecting land bridge in which only appreciation and memory were required to enjoy the moment. As simple as that. Playing and singing *Rubber Ball* by Bobby Vee could be just as enjoyable for me as nailing a difficult Django piece (a statement that could have Gypsy Jazzers spitting out their cornflakes).

LONNIE LEE
AND THE LEEMEN

One afternoon in 1998, after mainly playing in jazz and big bands for 18 years, I got a fairly desperate phone call from Chuck Morgan, a great Māori musician. Chuck had got himself double booked. He was up in the Hunter Valley playing guitar at a wedding while he was also supposed to be at Rooty Hill RSL playing with Lonnie Lee and the Leemen. He asked if I could fill in for him. There were apparently panic stations all round as club auditorium gigs required turning up hours before the concert started for sound checks and going through the charts with the main act and support act, in this case a female singer.

Due to the late notice, I arrived about half an hour before the downbeat but handled the charts and played well for both the support and Lonnie Lee. I also really enjoyed playing rock and roll again as it was my home base. A few weeks later, Lonnie asked me to join permanently so for the next 12 years I was one of the Leemen.

Lonnie and Suzanne, his wife, manager and caretaker of business, ran a good outfit and he was a genuine legend of Australian rock and roll being there at the start along with Alan Dale, Johnny O'Keefe and Col Joye. He also took care of himself, was a fine singer and prided himself on always having a quality lineup with the Leemen. The fact that I succeeded the great Chuck Morgan only emphasises this.

We played at various rock and roll festivals and many shows in club auditoriums. A polished show was always presented at these venues and Lonnie was well loved by his many fans. He always made a point of meeting them at the end of every show. As the Leemen were all readers as well as rock and rollers we also backed many other Australian rock and roll singers on the bill with Lonnie, including Johnny Devlin, Normie Rowe, Judy Stone, Ray Hoff, Alan Dale and the DeKroo Brothers. It was a thrill for me to actually work with these people, legends all of them.

In the 12 years with Lonnie two lineups really stand out for me. First, Mike Gubb on piano, Bob Randall on bass and Merv Dick on drums, along with me on guitar. Second, Warren Morgan on piano, Brian Deane on bass and Leon Isaacson on drums. This second lineup featured three genuine Australian music legends. While Brian and I were the journeymen, the other two legends apart from Lonnie were Warren 'Pig' Morgan who played with Chain, Billy Thorpe and John Paul Young and Leon Isaacson who played with Dig Richards, Winifred Attwell and many others. In fact, his feature number with the Leemen was *She Wears My Ring* and, of course, he played on the original O'Keefe recording. At times during these shows, I would just turn around, look at them and think ... Wow!

For quite a few years Lonnie Lee and the Leemen appeared at the Wintersun music festival in Coolangatta, a rock and roll extravaganza full of great bands, vintage cars and all sorts of rock and roll memorabilia. At one of these, I saw a really handsome young couple, dressed to the nines in impeccable 50's clothes and pushing a pram with their baby inside. The pram was shaped like a Chevrolet. At these festivals, Elvis impersonators abounded. I remember an old joke/ observation. A few years after Elvis died in 1978, there were 240 Elvis impersonators worldwide. In 10 years, that number had grown to about 5,000. On that trajectory by the year 2030, one-in-three people in the world will be an Elvis impersonator.

Lonnie regularly changed his show. He would vary his many hits around the number ones which would always be played. And he also paid tribute to other singers with nice versions of their songs ... Johnny O'Keefe, The Everly Brothers and Johnny Ray. Also, in time, the Leemen would play the first set in the show, replacing the various support acts. After all we were a pretty good self-contained support act and these sets were hugely enjoyable for us.

In 2006, a big rock and roll tour was organised called 'The Last of the Lee Gordon Big Shows'.

It starred Bobby Vee and his band, Crash Craddock and his band, Lesley Gore and her band, the DeKroo Brothers and Lonnie Lee and the Leemen. A financial failure but an amazing experience to tour around Australia with these big names. I was a bit shy but spoke briefly with Bobby Vee and Crash Craddock and the Leemen got on very well with Crash's backing band, a very friendly bunch of good 'ole' boys. I remember chatting with Leslie Gore and her telling me about a new song she had just recorded back in the States. She said it was written by Marvin and produced by Quincy. She meant of course Marvin Hamlisch and Quincy Jones. Music Royalty.

The Leemen started off these shows with an instrumental hit by the original Leemen, back in 1961, called *Johnny Guitar*, and this time featuring me. A proud moment indeed. These American musicians (all excellent by the way) were not exactly effusive in their praise but I did notice a few of them checking out the Leemen as we played this opening number. So as the old song says, *'I don't want to hang up my rock 'n' roll shoes.'*

Lonnie Lee and me on stage circa 2005.

Lonnie Lee and the Leemen 2000: (l to r), Pete Forrell, keyboards - Lonnie
- Merv Dick, drums - Bob Randall, bass guitar and me.

The Leemen lineup in 2009: (l to r), me - Leon Isackson, drums - Lonnie
- Warren Morgan, keyboards - Brian Deane, bass guitar.

Midway through my tenure with the Leemen, my first marriage with Linda wound up and, a few years later, I married Rose, Baoshan Yao, in Wuhan, China. Life stumbles on as they say and it is probably preferable to live in interesting times. Linda loved music and Rose was a good dancer, so music was never far away.

One day, on my first trip to China, Rose and I were strolling down by the Yangtze River, which intersects Wuhan. A Chinese band with traditional Chinese instruments were playing to a small crowd and Rose somehow roped me in to playing one of their stringed instruments to accompany a singer and then play an improvisation. I knew Chinese music was often in the Western pentatonic (five note) scale so I did my best and somehow it came out pretty good. Everyone was pleased. It seemed as if everyone in Wuhan loved to sing and dance.

On a bus we caught, (impossibly crowded, as Wuhan, while smaller in size than Sydney, is a city of 10 million people), the bus driver was singing for the entire journey with a tuneful and melodic voice. At family gatherings in restaurants, someone is always likely to get up and sing unaccompanied, so when it came to me, I'd usually sing *Road To Gundagai*.

Speaking of restaurants, whether cheap or expensive, or in people's homes as their guest, the food is superb. It is also 'chilli central' for those who like spicy. And for breakfast everyone goes out to the street vendors for a Wuhan specialty, spicy hot and dry noodles with some deep fried but light bread and Soya milk, warm in winter, cool in summer.

Looking back to growing up in Glebe there was one, then two Chinese restaurants with the amazing experience of eating bananas deep-fried in batter with ice cream. This is a rich culture which has been doing this continually for thousands of years. I also like Greek food and Lebanese food, again rich cultures that have been doing this continually for thousands of years

Bob took this photo in early 1974 in the early days of UBB at Newnes. Left to right Kate Kennington, Warwick Kennington under the hat Kathy James, Uncle Tony and young Jessica pondering a middle earth size mushroom - - ah do we eat this or do we eat it ?

With Rose in Wuhan in 2008.

MODERN RETRO SOUNDS ...
my life as an eclectic!
THE GENTLEMAN CALLERS/
RON CRAIG STUDIOS

From 2007 to 2012, The Gentleman Callers, a nice little guitar, bass and drums trio, with all three singing, would convene every week at drummer, Brett Rose's house at Lane Cove, to work on new songs. The band was bass player Peter Moloney's idea, playing classic 1960's pop songs with a different approach, often a reggae feel.

This sounded pretty good to me as I had long been a reggae fan and 60's songs were right up my alley. I did manage to introduce a few original songs, some co-written with singer, ukulele player and painter Carol Ruff, aka Coral Reef. We even managed to record two CDs at Brett's makeshift shed/recording studio. Brett was the engineer; Peter mixed the songs and they were mastered at Ron Craig's Delta Studios at Epping.

A special mention to Ron Craig (also a top guitarist) as both my first solo album in 2002 and Uncle Bob's Band's first reunion album in 2004 were recorded there as well. Both were exceptionally well-engineered and mixed by Ron, and the Uncle Bob's Band CD includes some of the finest, sound-wise and playing-wise, UBB recordings ever. But when UBB arrived and set up on the first night of recording, we noticed something odd in the studio. It was still set up from the previous night's recording by a jazz band from the 'cutting edge' side of the spectrum and they had attached nude photos of women on the music stands. Ron told us they did this to boost their testosterone levels while playing. The look on his face was just as bemused as ours. But, as distracting as these photos were, we had work to do.

THE MURRAY HILLBILLIES

A recent development has me playing string bass in an acoustic band led by Murray Hill. This band plays old time country music and features a couple of country music stalwarts in Colin Watson on guitar and Gary Brown on dobro. Murray plays guitar and sings and Ian, a stonemason by trade, is on mandolin. Playing songs by Roy Acuff, Jimmie Rodgers and Hank Williams, this is country retro and royalty and I really enjoy doing the simple but groovy bass lines with such esteemed company. We play at some of the monthly concerts held by the Sydney Bluegrass Society, all delightfully acoustic and full of enthusiasts.

JOHN and YUKI

For many years now I've been playing with bassist John Mackie and singer/pianist Yuki Kumigai. They both share my wide musical leanings and we play anything from jazz, 'trad' to modern, to country, to rock and roll and beyond. Nothing is off limits and therefore is an ongoing enjoyment. This lineup has never recorded but is well YouTubed and we occasionally augment the trio with drums and tenor sax to play at some clubs for dancers.

JAZZWEST

A mixture of 1930's swing jazz, Bob Wills Western swing and cowboy songs, JazzWest is Graham Griffith on pedal steel, Jenny Griffith on lead vocal and rhythm guitar, me on lead guitar and occasional vocals, and a pool of bass players and sometimes drums if there is a dancing crowd. The band is based around twin pedal steel and guitar lines, in harmony or unison and therefore a lot of homework and rehearsing. This is an aspect of playing music that many people don't think about. Good music just doesn't happen. It can, of course, at times of pure inspiration but most of the time, playing live music is the tip of the iceberg. There is an enormous amount of homework ice beneath the surface. Unpaid, unseen, perhaps under-appreciated but essential.

COOL BRITANNIA

Cool Britannia was a short lived but very enjoyable band that played British pop/rock songs from 1965 to 1975. We didn't play any Beatles as there were plenty of those tribute type bands around, invariably dressed in Sgt. Pepper outfits et al. (actually we did have 'George' and 'Ringo' from one of these tribute bands) but we did play some Cream, Stones, Kinks, Small Faces, Spencer Davis Group, Who, Hollies, plus others. Marcus Phelan and I did the two guitar parts, while former 60's guitar hotshot, Wayne Rountree, played electric bass, with Jeff Fitzgerald on lead vocal, Neil Rankin on drums and Darren Richards on keyboards. This was a marvellous band and I finally got to play some great 60's songs properly with a top-notch band and we recorded a few of them (which can be found on YouTube). These are audio-only and may be hard to locate as there appear to be numerous Cool Britannias (as there appear to be numerous Gentleman Callers) but look out for *Brown Sugar, He Ain't Heavy He's My Brother, All Day And All Of The Night, Band On The Run* and *Keep On Running.*

ERIC HOLROYD'S FIVE PENNIES

In the early 2000s, Yorkshireman/trumpeter, Eric Holroyd, put together this band based on the late 20's Chicago hot jazz group, Red Nichols Five Pennies, with Eric doing the Nichols trumpet part and Geoff Power doing the Miff Mole trombone part. I was pleased as punch to be cast as Eddie Lang in this lineup and my feature was playing Lang's solo guitar version of *Jeanine I'll dream of Lilac Time*, a charming turn-of-the-century song (19th into 20th), which was a favourite of my maternal grandmother, Elsie Mullins. I am very pleased to see that a revived interest in Eddie Lang can be found nowadays on YouTube as he was the first great jazz guitarist before Django, Charlie Christian and Wes Montgomery became the style's main innovators.

THEM WERE THE DAYS ...

Some things which I don't think exist much anymore but which were quite ubiquitous in the 1980's and 1990's were jazz trios (clarinet, double bass and guitar) playing on harbour cruises around Sydney harbour. These functions, corporate, wedding or presentation nights, were well paid and enjoyable gigs for bands, who were also well-fed and watered (wined and beered). And the beauty of the sunset on the harbour never lost its stunning appeal no matter how many times you saw it. For these jobs, the bands weren't expected to put on a show, just provide some background music and atmosphere, with occasional dancing. This meant we could just play our favourite jazz standards in a nice relaxing setting. What a way to work! This was also the time when just about all weddings had the same sort of jazz trio, playing away in the corner at restaurants and function centres, my favourite one being at Taronga Zoo which had THE most amazing view of the harbour, city skyline, bridge, and behind it, glorious sunset you could possibly imagine.

We were workers just like the caterers and waiting staff but, unlike them, musicians were able to have a drink (only on rare occasions did we hear about musos behaving badly in this regard). Playing music remains the only job I know of where the first thing you do after setting up is to go and grab a beer.

COLOURFUL RACING IDENTITIES

'Colourful racing identities' is a Sydney term, originally used to describe underworld figures, but I am using it in a friendly, self-deprecating way, common to musicians, to describe some characters and eccentrics in the music game. Here are some I can recall, and the mould was thrown away a few times with this lot.

Jesse Melrose, a music historian and true eccentric with great knowledge of early music styles; when and where they were recorded, and the musicians who played them. I once complimented him on the hat he was wearing. He ended up giving it to me along with his entire suit.

Mort Fist, a legendary figure in country music circles, both in Sydney and later in Tamworth. He was a genuine music aficionado, heavily involved in the Tamworth Country Music Festival, with his finger on the country pulse. He liked a beer and went way too soon and was sadly missed.

Peter Knox, played for a while with the Battersea Heroes, but best known for his outlandish performances, along with Frank Butler, in the 69'ers and later, as Izzy Foreal, with the Zarsoff Brothers. Sporting long black hair and a Frank Zappa moustache his onstage exploits were both musical and outrageous.

Paul Madigan, Melbourne singer and guitarist, was an interesting one-of-a-kind, who fronted a band called Paul Madigan and the Humans, which had quite a few luminaries in its ranks … Freddy Strauks, drummer from Skyhooks, Ross Hannaford and Wayne Duncan from Daddy Cool and Ed Bates, guitarist from the Sports. I occasionally sat in with the band and was given the pleasing title of Honorary Human. Paul wrote some great songs and lyrics, my favourite being about a girl he took on a date ... 'She had two cappuccinos and three tartufos ... Now you know where all my money goes.'

Peter Lillie was the legendary underground Melbourne guitarist and bandleader, and responsible for such great outfits as The Pelaco Bros and The Autodrifters. He was also famous as the 'After Dinner Moose,' who appeared at various T F Much Ballroom shows in Melbourne and wrote a classic Australian song *The Birth Of The Ute.*

No mention of characters from music would be complete without Mic Conway. Known by some as 'Mr Vaudeville' Mic Conway can be both out of his time and timeless simultaneously. From his days with Captain Matchbox Whoopee Band, to rock singer with the Matchbox Band, to his National Junk Orchestra and school performer, there never has been anyone quite like him. And all of us who have ever played with him still laugh at his on-stage corny jokes, knowing full well that we would never get away with telling them ... not like 'Mr Vaudeville' can.

Another original is Terry Darmody from OBH and UBB. Like Mic Conway, it is hard to think of anyone else quite like him. Jim Conway has long been revered as a harmonica player and Terry is up there with him in terms of melodic phrasing on a blues harp. Nowadays, Terry is deeply into Christianity and Gospel music but has not forgotten his secular roots in music and has recently released a limited-edition CD called 'Long Way from Home,' which I think is his crowning achievement, and is helped in no small measure by the contributions of two genuine A Grade musicians, in Marcus Holden (anything strings) and Don Hopkins (anything keyboards). I play double bass and a bit of guitar, and Adam Barnard is on drums. Son of the great Bob Barnard, and nephew of the great Len Barnard, he has the natural gift. This CD of Terry's features a version of Dylan's *Dear Landlord* which, with its rollicking feel, knocks on the door of The Basement Tapes, which, for those familiar with these seminal recordings by Dylan and the Band, is one of the beating hearts of music.

Bob McGowan … if ever there was anyone who you would want to see reach a venerable age it was Bob; 73 was way too soon to lose him. I have already written about Bob as a musician but now I want to write a few words about the man.

Bob was the only person I knew without any jealousy, pointed put-downs, narrow mindedness or any of the bullshit every one of us occasionally succumbs to. He was universally loved and he could see through anyone's foibles without making a big deal of it. This is a rare gift and he was a rare man, and all of us who knew him well are fortunate indeed.

I fondly recall his occasional slide nights where we would sit entranced with Bob's close-up nature photography. We might walk on grass but there is a magical world down there beneath our feet which few of us would contemplate. So in photography, as in music, Bob could recognise a natural inner realm of wonder which only requires an interested imagination.

During the 70's my favourite Australian bands were Daddy Cool and the La De Das but special mention for a band that recorded, in my opinion, the greatest Australian rock album ever Product Of A Broken Reality. The band was Company Caine, led by another colourful identity, Gulliver Smith. This album is a masterpiece, featuring memorable songs, playing and arrangements as well as distinctive vocals, full of character. The guitar playing by Russell Smith, is first class and puts him just after my top three from the 70's … Ross Hannaford, Kevin Borich and Bob McGowan.

Now that I've begun, I may as well list more of my favourite musicians. For a start anyone from the Cafe Society Orchestra and Uncle Bob's Band.

On drums, the late Alan Gilbert and the late Bob Gillespie and the very much with us, Adam Barnard. The two Lauries, Bennett and Thompson can take a bow as well. On guitar the late Chuck Morgan and, still active, Graham Conlon, who, apart from being masterful on guitar, is also a top-notch bloke. And of course the great Ian Date, up there with the virtuosos.

On electric bass, my favourite has always been John Taylor from UBB (likewise Warwick Kennington on drums). For double bass, apart from Dave Clayton, there is the late Deiter Vogt and the late 'Smedley' (Chris Qua) for being comfortable and swinging. John Mackie and Stan Valacos also fit this bill. For classy jazz soloing, Craig Scott and Dave Seidel are hard to beat.

There are so many others, on various instruments, that I'd need a second book to list them all, and perhaps there should be more musical memoirs from others written to complete this list … along with countless other stories from the rich tapestry.

Left to right - Dave Clayton, the eyes have it, Al Meadows with fez, Al Ward assuming command, Dennis Sutherland (drums) and me awaiting orders.

GUITARS AND AMPS

Over the years, I've played in quite a few quality bands of different styles so I suppose you could say I had to be a good player to do that. But to be honest I've often struggled with fast tempos (I'm no match for the Gypsy Jazzers) and what I've noticed over all these years is that most compliments that come my way are about the great sound that I get, so that comes down to equipment, guitars and amps, based on simplicity and quality.

Firstly, the best sound for guitars is valve amps and for me that means Fender and Vox. Valve amps have that basic depth of tone and warmth that suits guitars. Transistor amps, digital amps and modelling amps have all sorts of weird and wonderful sounds with knobs, buttons, bells and whistles. Lots of different sounds except the right one. I've yet to see a valve guitar amp being advertised as having a genuine transistor sound. As long as guitar amps are made you are never going to see that. However, transistor amps are more suitable for electric bass and better for keyboards and PAs while some jazz guitar players like to use them.

The only time I stepped outside this strict strategy was with the Battersea Heroes when, after originally playing my Jason guitar through my Fi-Sonic amp, we all had Dynacord amps. (Bob and I continued to use these 80w amps in UBB). These were hybrid amps like Musicman and had a solid-state preamp and a valve power section with 1x ECC83 and 2x EL34. Made in Germany but with Australian Etone speakers in a Freedman cabinet, they actually sounded good when cranked, but in late UBB I got my first Fender, a 20w Blackface Deluxe Reverb. Welcome to the soul of tone.

On Sgt. Peppers, the Beatles played their guitars through a mixture of Vox amps, hybrid, solid state and valve resulting in some iconic sounds. I prefer the guitar sound from Rubber Soul which was Fender Stratocasters through Vox AC 30's, which they took out of storage and re-introduced after using giant Vox AC 100's for the Help album. These, they decided (or George Martin and engineer Norman

Smith decided) were too loud for the studio. Also, by this stage, Fender had joined Vox as Beatles amplification, first with a 1963 blonde Bassman for both guitar and bass, then two 1966 Showman amps for John and George (used on the Revolver album) then later with a Deluxe and a couple of Twins. I wonder how many people know that the classic guitar sound on the Clapton album, 'Layla,' was Eric Clapton and Duane Allman playing through Fender Champs … all of 5 watts! Valve Heaven!

All of this detail is just to emphasise that amps are just as important as guitars (and hands) in creating classic sounds and, in many cases, the smaller the better.

I still have a Fender Deluxe Reverb (Original 1967 blackface) and a Vox AC 15 (one of the last Vox amps made in England in 2003 before production was moved to China) but nowadays I mainly use a Fender Pro Junior 1V, 15 watts, and a Vox AC 4, 4 watts, both being light, portable and great sounding. The Pro Junior also has just two knobs, one for volume and one for tone, just like my first amp, the Goldentone.

For those who are interested, the Vox has 1 x 12AX7 valve for the preamp and 1 x EL84 valve for the output. The Fender has two of each. Generally speaking, the sound of Vox amps is EL84 output valves while the Fender sound is 6L6 output valves for the bigger amps, and 6V6 for the smaller amps. The Pro Junior, having 2x EL84, is a nice mixture of the two companies.

Just as important as valves are speakers. My 67 Deluxe Reverb's original 12" Oxford speaker shuffled off its magnetic coil in 2007 and was replaced with a 12" Ceramic Jensen (now made in Italy). The AC 15 has two 10" Ceramic Eminence speakers. The Pro Junior has a 10" Alnico Jensen while the AC 4 has a 10" Ceramic Celestion. Alnico and Ceramic refer to the alloys used in the magnets of speakers and are said to have different sound qualities, but they both sound pretty good to me. Jensen and Celestion are just as reputable brand names as Fender and Vox.

Next my guitar … 1968 Gibson ES 330 semi acoustic with one (neck) P90 pickup. (I long ago took out the bridge pickup). Not only does this guitar sound great and play great but it looks great. I've had people coming up to the stage when I play to take a photo of it and hardly a gig goes by without someone commenting on this walnut brown beauty which I've been playing since 1971. The laminated finish, now cracked and faded and worn away on the back of the neck, shows its age well, comfortable in its skin and happy to have seen the mileage, and if you ever hear about an old guitar in mint condition, that probably means it hasn't been played much, making it a pristine but sad guitar.

B.B. King had *Lucille*, George Harrison had *Rocky*, Neil Young had *Old Black* and Willie Nelson had *Trigger* … I had *Gertrude!*

I also occasionally play an Epiphone Casino, which is exactly the same as a 330. Why have two of the same guitar? Well, the Beatles played Casinos. John, George and Paul all played one and after Lennon's Rickenbacker and George's Gretsch and 12 string Rickenbacker, the Casinos became classic Beatles guitars. Also Gertrude is never taken on a plane.

I don't use any pedals and have never put a capo on my guitar. As long as the basic sound is full and clean with just a slight edge to it from just pushing those valves a bit, then I'm away.

For acoustic guitar in jazz bands, I play a late 30's Harmony Cremona archtop F hole guitar with little sustain on the top strings but a classic chordal sound for rhythm. Also a Gitane round sound hole guitar; a copy of the famous Selmer guitar played by Django. Made in China, this is a delight to play and is never in its case but at arms-length from my spot on the lounge.

For strings on electric guitar I go for Ernie Ball Power Slinky's, 011 to 049. Most rock guitarists prefer 010 to 046, a bit lighter and easier to bend, and jazz players prefer 012 to 052, a more solid sound for chords but not very suitable for bending strings. So, my preferred gauge straddles both camps like Talos with his bronze feet on both headlands (only film buffs will get this reference and I stress it's only imagery, not a declaration).

1978, in the Matchbox Band with Pete Muhleisen, bass and Stephen Cooney, guitar. Judging by the moustache this was just after my failed audition for the Village People.

My double bass is also a talking point. It is an 'original Hopf,' made by Hofner in the 1940's. Apparently it was their gypsy model and is a blonde cutaway with strips of tortoise shell along its sides and Art Deco Sound holes. I've never seen another string bass like it and although it is plywood rather than solid wood, the sound is rich and deep and, like Gertrude, is always commented on, from 'sexy' to 'Salvador Dali.'

So, I can consider my instruments and amps the real stars - I just try and use them properly. Good tone and groove is the aim … always.

I suppose in philosophical musical terms there are two basic camps; play the song or play the instrument. In the first camp, where I pitch my tent, the musician uses the instrument to play the song, giving it top priority whether in a faithful recreation or in a different but respectful approach. In the second camp, the musician uses the song to play the instrument to display his wares. This is not showing off, just showcasing a formidable technique (the realm of the virtuoso) and is usually expected and appreciated by their fans. And while great songs can be badly played by anyone, the more confident and professional usually get the balance right.

I've always considered taking solos as interrupting my guitar playing as my main musical focus has been putting in place a rhythmic groove and feel to compliment a good song. Always with the best sounding chords. The chord melody style of Django and Wes Montgomery are the pinnacle. For bluesy single string playing, Eric Clapton is my favourite while Chuck Berry wrote the rock and roll guitar book as well as being poet laureate. John, George, Keith and Brian knew how to groove and bring a song alive. And distinctive players like Charlie Christian, Ry Cooder and Robbie Robertson set up their own niche. But no mention of guitar players is complete without Robert Johnson standing down at the crossroads making his deal with the devil.

A notion that occurred to me quite a few years back was that there was a correlation between playing in a band and playing in a team sport like football/soccer. In a tactical sense, the bass player and drummer are defenders, rarely going forward in attack but concentrating on holding the fort and providing a solid base on which to build. Chordal players, like pianists and guitarists, operate like a midfield playing 'from box to box;' that is, the middle third of the field. In front of them is the attacking third and behind is the defending third. It is often said in football that games are won or lost in midfield. If you win you attack, if you lose you defend.

Singers, lead instruments and soloists are up front, attacking players, hell-bent on scoring goals. In fact, that's all they are required to do. They are the stars, usually with the biggest egos and the most photogenic. They are also the ones that young players aspire to be when they grow up, whether it be Hank Marvin playing guitar, Elvis singing or Lionel Messi scoring goals.

Cole Buchanan sketched this while watching me play in a jazz trio.

PERILS OF THE ROAD

I am lucky to be alive. Ain't no doubt about that. The dangers of long-distance driving with touring bands are real and present. But also in the 70's a further concern for musicians was the over-zealous antics of law enforcement, when long haired, dope smoking hippies were considered a real menace to society. As far as I can remember none of us had guns or knives. As for robbing banks, or break and entering, well, we were all too stoned for any of that.

Speaking of this, in 1971 the Battersea Heroes used to play quite a bit at Joseph's Coat, a music venue in the city down by Darling Harbour. It was our usual practice to adjourn to Bob's panel van in the break and smoke some Buddha sticks which were very strong. However, on this particular night someone had given us some equally strong Hash Cookies to eat which, in the break, were starting to take effect. As we were sitting in Bob's van, the police knocked on the closed window, no doubt seeing a bunch of long hairs in a panel van full of smoke and rubbing their hands at our subsequent arrest. But when Bob unwound the window it was apparent, even to these guys, that we were merely smoking cigarettes. On top of that, Bob had a can of beer in his hand. The police had to go on their merry way while we remained extremely stoned, sitting in the van. It took us a while to laugh but laugh we did.

Anyway, getting back to the road, I had a number of lucky escapes.

The first was in the Battersea Heroes. I was driving Bob's Ford Transit Van around 6am with Bob, Kathy and possibly young Jessica sleeping in the back, when I was suddenly awakened by cars blasting their horns. I had fallen asleep and veered right across the, fortunately, straight road, onto the gravel on the other side, with oncoming cars blasting their horns at me. A lucky escape indeed and *mea culpa.*

The second was on tour with the Matchbox Band. I was driving south down the coast to Newcastle for our next gig. Also in the car were Mic Conway, Peter Muhleisen and Louis McManus. We were going up a steep hill when suddenly the car began swerving and sliding. An oil slick perhaps. There was a very steep embankment to our left and any descent down there would have been catastrophic but I managed to correct the car, coming to a stop a few feet from the edge. Shaken, I was given a vote of confidence by the others and continued driving, albeit at a very sedate tempo, although Mic kept saying we would be late for the gig. We were only slightly late … better than never.

Third, a very tragic one. This day, in early 1979, the Matchbox Band had two gigs, one in Melbourne and the other down south in the Mornington Peninsula. There was copious alcohol at both gigs and at the end of the second one I was well-sozzled. I fell in with this girl and she and her friends suggested we go to a party. We crammed into a smallish sports car with a, fortunately, hard roof. There were three in the front seat and four of us in the back.

The driver, a young girl aged about 21, was drunk as well. I sat directly behind her with one of the girls on my knees. No seat belts were used and her driver's door, apparently, was not closed properly. Suddenly the car started swerving, she lost control and in trying to correct the steering she fell out the door, which had opened. The car continued on, driverless and began to roll. I remember two things … this roll happened in slow motion and I remained physically relaxed due to the alcohol. I came to under a bush at the side of the road. I had been thrown out of the back window. The car itself had stopped, upright, narrowly missing a large tree. I don't know how long I was out, perhaps momentarily, but I saw that the others were all dazed and bleeding, while my only injury was a bump on the head. We then noticed the body lying in the middle of the road about 40 yards away. It was the driver, the 21-year-old girl. I went up to her and felt her pulse for any sign of life. She was dead.

Shocked and instantly sober, we positioned ourselves to stop any approaching cars and the ambulance and police arrived in due course. I will never forget that moment when I saw the poor girl fall out of the car, a split second forever etched. Nor will I ever understand how the rest of us survived.

These were the days before random breath testing and I remember that in the years before this tragic occurrence, whenever we were out drinking, I was usually the designated drunk driver, as I could drive in a slow and careful manner while quite inebriated. Or at least better than the others. Youthful madness or more correctly, stupidity. But once you are in a fatal car accident, you realise that in a split second, all could be lost.

During the 1978 Soapbox Circus tour up the east coast to Cairns and back we had a truck smash just outside of Bellingen, our next concert. There were no fatalities or injuries but a lot of equipment was destroyed. The bush telegraph went out to the Bellingen community who helped out and the show went on. Our guitars were in a car and so were not involved and a Fender and Vox amp apparently bounced harmlessly on the road and still worked. However many of the theatre props were demolished as were most of the drums and, particularly sadly for Peter Muhleisen, his 100-year-old German double bass was in pieces. I remember him walking through the wreckage and picking up pieces of an irreplaceable musical instrument with a look of sadness and disbelief.

In 1979, after I left the Matchbox Band, there was another truck smash and this time Ivan, one of the road crew, lost his life. The following phrase is often trotted out to honour someone lost to us but in Ivan's case it is impeccably true. He really was one of the nicest people you could ever meet. Endlessly smiling, friendly and happy. A gentleman and a true delight. And a young man tragically lost as was the young girl. Such is the peril of the rock and roll road.

The Hume Highway, which connects Sydney and Melbourne, has seen a lot of rock and roll traffic going back to the early days of the genre, where it probably started with cars with large boots, and then station wagons. In the 1970's, this was upgraded to Kombi vans and Ford Transit vans, which would be filled with drums, PA speaker boxes, a few amps and guitars and probably three musicians in the front seat while one slept on top of the speakers in the back.

Before its upgrades and bypasses, the old Hume Highway would wind up and over Razorback Mountain, south-west of Sydney. It was quite a long ascent, and I remember on one trip back from Melbourne, the engine of our van was really struggling. It had barely made it up a few prior steep ascents so for Razorback Mountain the driver came up with a plan. At his signal, as the van slowed, the person in the passenger's seat and the one in the back would open their respective doors and jump out. This loss of weight would give the van a boost to get to the top. I was the one in the back and we both jumped out and ran after the van, meeting it at the top of the hill. I'm not making this up. These were the days when black Gaffa tape held everything together from guitar case handles to shoes. There's no business like show business.

MUSICAL FRAGMENTS

Well, I've covered a fair bit of musical ground in these chapters so far. I've kept things pretty short in the interest of editing and sticking to a general theme of highlighting some great bands and musicians with whom I've played. My reflections on them have not been exhaustive and tell-all. There have been a few bad moments and memories over the years and a few dogs that should remain sleeping. Music is an enjoyable pastime so who wants to hear that sort of stuff. As I have said, enjoyment is its aim and destination.

But I think a few more isolated musical memories of mine might be in order.

In summer, early 1964, age eleven-and-a-half, I saw, up close, my first rock and roll band. This was Ray Brown and the Whispers playing in a small hall at one of Sydney's southern beaches. I stood outside the open window at the back of the hall and directly inside the band was set up. Lead singer, two guitars, bass and drums. I distinctly remember two things ... they were all wearing black Beatle boots with those Cuban heels, and also, the warm smell coming from the hot valves working hard in their black piggyback amps. Piggyback meaning an enclosed speaker box, on top of which was the head or amp top, powered by valves, inside of which electrons were doing their thing.

I've already mentioned seeing the Beatles at the Sydney Stadium in June 1964. But my next memorable concert was at Festival Hall in Melbourne in late 1968. This was singer Paul Jones, The Who (then smashing guitars and amps, and headliners) and the amazing Small Faces, who were as exciting as live rock and roll could get.

In 1971, a few of us in the Battersea Heroes went to see the Stones at Randwick Racecourse. This was the second classic lineup with Mick Taylor, although I am envious of those who saw the first classic lineup with Brian Jones at the Hordern Pavilion in 1965. My father, who took me to see the Beatles in 1964, drew the line at the Rolling Stones.

Just before turning 18, in June 1970, I went, with other underage male and female friends from Glebe to the Sydney nightclub, Chequers, to see the Four Tops. They were sensational. After the show we were standing at the bar and turned around to see Duke from the Four Tops standing there. He was well over six feet tall and we all gazed at this impeccably dressed and fabulous looking black man. Being young and not very hip, we asked him all sorts of dumb questions which he answered very politely with great patience and manners. It was not the last time I would sort of freeze in front of stars but I always remembered the class of Duke from the Four Tops.

In April 1972, age 19, and into my second year with the Battersea Heroes, I went to the Hordern Pavilion. We were living close by at Cook Road, Centennial Park and our new bass player, Bob Dames's wife, worked for the advertising company that handled Gough Whitlam's Labor Party campaign. So it was that I became part of the chorus singing the 'It's Time' commercial. That's me at the bottom right hand corner - the gawky looking 19-year-old with long black hair and wearing a light coloured jumper. You can see Bob Dames there as well. Also, briefly, standing beside me, Battersea Heroes' drummer, Dennis Burke.

It's Time was sung by Alison McCallum, and the chorus line was full of TV personalities like Bobby Limb, Dawn Lake, Jimmy Hannan, John Dease senior, actor Jack Thompson, Col Joye, Little Pattie and many others. A few months later, before the election, I received a personally signed thank you letter from Gough Whitlam, Leader of the Opposition, thanking me for my generous co-operation in filming the party commercial. This letter is framed and remains a prized possession, displayed prominently on the wall at home.

It's Time commercial, 1972, I am in the blue.
Courtesy National Film and Sound Archive.

Paradise Road, directed by Bruce Beresford, 1997. I am in the black.

In May 1996, some members of the Cafe Society Orchestra spent a few days filming the first three riveting minutes of the Bruce Beresford film Paradise Road. This was filmed at the Marrickville Town Hall in Sydney, decked out to look like the Raffles Bar in Singapore, circa 1942. In the film, we were called the Herbert Cecil Orchestra, and Julie Anthony was cast as the chanteuse. It was a great experience with big stars, Glen Close, Francis McDormand, Jennifer Ehle (from Pride and Prejudice) and our own Cate Blanchett.

Three minutes on film took three days shooting and I was fascinated to observe how big budget movies were made, from the technicians and equipment to the extras and to the stars, who had their own caravans to retire to in between scenes. A certain protocol, unspoken but understood, was in place for the main star, Glenn Close, in which it seemed only the director was permitted to talk to her. However, she seemed nice and once when she was entering the hall and I passed her on my way out she smiled at me.

Once, in between scenes, I was sitting near the stage and Jennifer Ehle came along with an apple and sat down. She asked if I had a knife so she could cut it but I could only, lamely, answer 'sorry no.' I wish I could have thought of more witty repartee to say to the beautiful Miss Elizabeth Bennett, but like Mr Darcy, I was a bit tongue-tied.

There is a lot of sitting around and waiting for scenes to be set up. All the extras know this and bring along a book. We musicians, a couple of times, decided to go down to the nearby Marrickville pub for a couple of beers. Bruce Beresford, the director and a pretty cool guy, didn't throw a fit, merely sending down a runner to get us when our next scene was on.

Musos are a funny lot. We have to be. Anyone who plays in a band knows that the music game is one where, when one door closes, another one is slammed shut in your face. To get anywhere in music you need a lot of talent but also a lot of luck (a single minded and determined promotional drive also helps, and probably a ruthless, 'take no prisoners' manager). Therefore, a sense of humour is not only an antidote but an acceptance of just how ridiculous the music game can be. There can be tears of rage, tears of grief and tears of joy. May as well laugh at it, and the artistic temperament as well for that matter.

So here's some muso humour ...

'We had the audience eating off their plates.'

'The band on before us was so bad the audience was still booing halfway through our set.'

'What do you throw a drowning guitarist? - His amplifier.'

'Nostalgia ain't what it used to b.'

'Our new album has sold under a million copies,'

- has just gone cardboard,'

- is heading down the charts with an anchor,'

'Yes she's a singer of some note. Exactly what note is yet to be determined.'

'Kenny G.? ... yeah, if I played like that I wouldn't give my second name either.'

A couple of twists on famous old songs ...

'Twas on a pile of debris that I found her.' (*Isle of Capri*)

'I'll be seizing you in all the old familiar places.' (*I'll Be Seeing You*)

There are others of course, outrageously funny, but not quite General Exhibition.

Vignettes from the bandstand ...

Eric Holroyd (trumpet) was sitting next to Paul Williams (tenor sax). After playing a solo, Paul sits down and Eric says, 'Ah, there's nothing like a good tenor sax solo - and that was nothing like a good tenor sax solo.' In the next song, Eric plays the solo but is not happy with it and sits down saying that it was the worst solo he'd ever played, to which Paul replies, 'Oh no, no, no, I've heard you play worse than that lots of times.'

Drummer Len Barnard was full of funny lines. 'That couple have been married so long they're into their second bottle of Tabasco ... I had the band on the Kon Tiki ... Giving someone like me Viagra would be like putting a new flagpole on a condemned building.'

One time, in The Cafe Society, Geoff Embleton pointed to me to take a rare guitar solo. Sitting next to me Len leant over and said, 'This is your big chance, don't stuff it up.' I began the solo laughing but regained my composure. The story goes that with Len in his last days in hospital, he was asked if he wanted to be buried or cremated to which he replied, 'Surprise me.'

At drummer Bob Gillespie's funeral, the service was over, the curtain closed and we expected the coffin to be removed. All of a sudden the sound of applause came through the sound system and the curtains opened with the coffin still there. Bob had arranged to give himself a curtain call.

Bass player Dieter Vogt was playing a trio job with clarinetist Paul Furniss and Māori guitarist, Chuck Morgan, when, in one of the breaks, someone came up and asked what the band's name was. Dieter looked around and said, in his Swiss accent, 'Dieter, Paul and Māori.'

Dieter and I were both football (soccer) fans. I actually played competition Over 35 and Over 45 football for 25 years, from the age of 43 to 68, with the West Ryde Rovers and Putney Rangers. At one World Cup, I said to Dieter, 'What about that German goalkeeper, Oliver Kahn. Hasn't he got a really strong looking German face?' Dieter replied, 'Yes, you 'vant' to hit it.'

The two Pauls are still with us, but Eric, Len, Bob, Dieter, 'Tappers', 'Smedley' and Chuck are all gone, along with many others, but the memory of their music and good humour lives on.

So there it is. For me, a life rich in music. I never made much money but spent my whole life doing what I was meant to do and that, in the absence of fame and fortune, is quite satisfying. A music lover from way back and a fortunate one at that and occasionally, in questionable moments, the guitarist who knows no shame.

In my more grandiose moments, I like to consider myself the most talented nobody in Australian music. However, I do realise there must be a Melbourne Cup field in this category. For anyone playing music, there are different levels ... beginners, amateurs, professionals, virtuosos and a very select genius group. From the start, everyone is a beginner. Amateurs can become lifelong enthusiasts while professionals try and make a living from the music game. Virtuosos are professionals with a heightened technical ability where competition is rife, but the handful of genius practitioners are the ones who inspire us all. And for them, to attain the highest level of musical beauty and creativity is the end goal.

So, for all the other talented nobodies around, remember, we follow the same path as those who occupy those few seats at the long table of the Musical Gods, up there on Mount Olympus. We won't sit and sup with them but we can enjoy the same musical journey.

And don't ask me what 'It's a Claude Rains gonna fall' means.

POSTSCRIPT

In October 2023, we finally got round to having a wake for Pete Nehill who died a couple of years previously, during the COVID lockdown years. It was, fittingly, a musical send-off and we made it a quality affair.

Dom O'Donnell, a good lad and fellow music lover, organised it and a wide range of music was played by Murray Hill, Terry Darmody, Gary Brown, Steve Darmody, Graham and Jenny Griffith and me. Music is a young man's game, and a young woman's game, but for a bunch of 70-something year olds who know what they're doing and have been doing it for over 50 years, there's hope yet!

JazzWest trio, December 2023: (l to r) Me, Jenny Griffith, Graham Griffith.
Senior citizens at work.

ACKNOWLEDGEMENTS

These recollections are all from my memory bank and as I approach my autumnal years I decided it was time to gather them as I, nowadays, can sometimes walk into a room but forget why. However, these musical memories remain fresh as a daisy and clear as a bell ... which may explain the ringing in my ears.

A big thank you goes to publisher Tom Thompson for his encouragement and faith in me and also to Elizabeth Butel whose expertise as editor whipped these rambling passages into shape.

Thanks also to Kathy James who provided some of the photos and the late cartoonist Cole Buchanan who sketched a cartoon while watching me play in a jazz trio. My thanks go to John Taylor for his posters and to the late Ian Shadwick for his photographs and cover.

WEBSITE LINKS

Re T-shirts: They are available as cool T Shirts. Check out posigns@bigpond.net.au

The Original Battersea Heroes album is available on DuMonde records (www.ozrecords.com.au)

Uncle Bob's Band CD's both original recordings from the 70's, later reunion CD's and 'Django Rock' are available on Discogs.

Also highly recommended is a compilation CD called Twenty Du Monde A Sides, rare 1970's OZ Rock also available on ozrecords.com.au. This features a lot of Martin Erdman's best recordings from 1969 to 1973. The Battersea Heroes have one song on this (we sound pretty groovy) and it's a good collection from that time featuring three songs from Flake, an impressive but somewhat forgotten band from the 70's.

Some of these CD's are also available from Red Eye Records in Sydney, located in York Street, near the Town Hall. Red Eye has an excellent selection of Australian music CD's and is highly recommended.

Printed in Australia
Ingram Content Group Australia Pty Ltd
AUHW010900100524
394194AU00001B/1